Investment Banking Interview Questions and Answers Prep Guide

(Complete with comprehensive 200 Questions and Answers)

Ace your technical questions and tell your unique story that will intrigue the MD despite your background.

By Chris J. Brodie

Contents

Introduction

Thank you for supporting my work. I am confident that the content in this book will help you get success in this highly competitive field. The investment banking field attracts the most hardworking and competitive people. Therefore, it is imperative that you get any advantage that you can get. I believe this guide is one of them.

As a veteran of the industry, I know what works and what doesn't. I have spent considerable time collecting information from my previous analyst hires and compiled the path of least resistance to get your foot in the door for that dream investment banking job.

This guide will help you to create your own action plan to get your foot in the door for the interviews. I will warn you now that it will be a grind, and it will test your willpower, but with all things that are good in life, you must fight for it.

If you have followed the action plan, I have no doubt in my mind that you will be offered a shot at an interview. The interview will be difficult, as it is an exercise to weed out strong candidates and get to the best of the best. The final part of this guide will concentrate on the interview. This guide has 200 interview questions listed and corresponding answers, being prepared with these interview questions and practicing answering them will give you a substantial leg up on your competition.

Yours Truly,

Chris J. Brodie

Is This for You?

Before we dive too deep into this guide, let's make sure an investment banking career path is right for you. I want to make sure that expectations and reality are aligned so that you won't be wasting time and effort chasing sometime that is not there.

Take a moment to reflect on why you want to pursue a career in investment banking. Found the reason why? Good.

Here are reasons why *not* to pursue an investment banking career:

- **You want work-life balance:** I can't believe I have to mention this, but I have seniors in college asking me about work-life balance in investment banking. The answer is NONE, not even on a VP level. If you want a job where you work 8-10 hours per day, never work weekends or stay late, and never get stressed out, investment banking will not be it.

- **You want to make a lot of money quickly:** It's a long haul; it takes a ton of work, and you have to sacrifice friends/family/hobbies along the way with no guarantee of success.

- **Your work will be of greater social good:** Nope! The reason you are hired is to make rich people even richer.

- **Just to prove that you can do it:** Once you "did it" and got through as an associate, then what? You will still hate your job.

- **Impress the opposite sex:** Are you serious? Trust me in saying that going to the best business school in the country and being an Investment Banker will not impress, at least not the ones you want to impress, anyway.

I've been mentoring students and professionals for a while, and I could think of a few reasons to genuinely pursue an investment banking career:

- **You are actually interested in work and can see yourself doing it for the long term:** Some people find financial analysis, valuation, and advising companies interesting and engaging; if this is you, great! You're set. Keep reading.

- **You want to gain the skill set and experience for other related jobs in the future:** Despite everything going against the finance industry, you will almost certainly learn more, and learn more quickly, in 2-3 years at a bank than you would in 99% of other jobs.

Craft Your Story

Knowing the reasons why you want to get into investment banking produces the basis for crafting your story. This is the response you give when you get asked questions such as "Walk me through your resume" or "Tell me about yourself." This story should not be more than 1-2 minutes long, and answers these three questions:

- What have you done before?
- Why investment banking, and why now?
- Why should we hire you?

Here's how to structure your story:

1. The "Beginning"
2. Your Finance "Spark"
3. Your Growing Interest
4. Why You're Here Today and Your Future

1. The ginning

Say where you grew up–if you're an undergrad or recent graduate, or where you went to university and where you started your career if you're more experienced.

Also, mention what you were planning to do before you became interested in finance (or before you developed an interest in the specific group with which you're interviewing).

2. Your Finance "Spark"

What made you interested in finance in the first place?

Were you working at a non-profit when it merged with another non-profit, which made you interested in the M and A process?

Did one of your parents start an ice cream truck business that needed to raise capital so it could add chocolate chip mint to its inventory?

Did you win an investing competition by picking a pharmaceutical stock that outperformed the market by 150%?

Naming specific people, places, and numbers while citing unusual experiences is one of the most powerful strategies here.

3. Your Growing Interest

Walk through your jobs, internships, and activities (if you're a student) and explain how each one led you in the direction of finance and investment banking specifically.

With each experience, mention something that you liked and something that you wanted to change.

4. Why You're Here Today and Your Future

You should state: "I'm interviewing here today because..." and spell it out explicitly.

Ideally, you will link this to your background: "I'm interviewing here today because I want to combine my background in strategy at retailers and knowledge of finance to become an adviser to consumer retail companies."

If you can't do that, talk about why you're interested in the deals this bank/group works on.

In the end, give some indication of your future plans by stating: "In the long term, I want to (explain your future plans), and I see this firm/group as the best way to get there because (point to their clients, deals, or other details)."

Example Story:

Sure. I grew up in China and attended high school in the U.S. and then began studying at the University of Chicago to learn more about finance while gaining a strong liberal arts background.

I became very interested in finance at a young age because my parents were both active day traders, and they did well trading natural resource and construction stocks just as the financial markets in China were opening up.

I did a double major in Math and Philosophy and then went back to China to work in wealth management at a local firm after my first year. I liked working in the financial markets and advising clients, but I wanted to work with more institutional clients and do more in-depth analysis.

So the year after that, I went to Hong Kong and worked in asset management at JP Morgan. I liked the institutional investors' focus and the more in-depth analytical work, but while I was working there, I got more interested in M and A because one of the companies I followed was acquired at a huge premium (over 100%).

So I started speaking with alumni and others in the investment banking industry and also learning more about the technical side—valuation and financial modeling—on my own. I want to do IB rather than asset management because you advise companies on decisions that impact their long-term business prospects instead of just "following" companies.

I'm here today because, in the future, I want to become a trusted adviser to companies with presences in both the US and China and advise on cross-border deals, leveraging my background in both countries and my experience in finance. I'm confident that your group is the best way for me to get there because of your track record of working on these types of deals."

How to Network Like a Pro

Now that your mind is set on becoming an investment banker, it is time for you to come up with a plan to access the right recruiting channels. There are many recruiting channels, some more obvious than others. The more obvious ones are campus recruitment and applying via the firm's website. These channels are obvious, and I won't be spending any time talking about them.

There are two approaches to networking that can be highly effective if done right. Before I get into it, I want to emphasize two things. First, these two methods may sound obvious, but the key is the proper implementation of it. Second, it is not a secret pill where you will get multiple interviews at different banks right away it will require work and will test your resolve.

There are two approaches to networking:

1. **Developing relationships:** You do this by conducting informational interviews and weekend trips, attending information sessions, and meeting bankers in any other way you can. It works well, and it can get you into an investment bank, but it takes a lot of time, and you need to start 6–12 months in advance of recruiting season.
2. **Cold-calling/cold-emailing:** Find lots of local boutique banks (or even PE firms or other finance firms), set aside an hour each day for cold-calling or cold-emailing, and don't give up until you get a good answer. This is more about persistence and consistency than "skill," though using the right tactics helps.

Developing Relationships

This strategy is more appropriate if you have 6-12 months of lead time, you have access to a solid alumni network, or you can otherwise get referrals to bankers through mutual connections.

Here are the steps:

1. **Make your list**

a. Start with alumni, family, friends, professional contacts, and anyone you meet at information sessions, and then expand into student groups, professional organizations, volunteer groups, and professors.

2. **Make the initial outreach**

    a. Email each contact to set up a 10-15 minute informational interview. Put your school and/or workplace and/or mutual connection in your subject, then introduce yourself and say how you found them in 1-2 sentences.

    b. Then, give 1-2 sentences on your previous work experience and propose a specific range of dates and times to speak with them or meet in person.

3. **Follow-up if you don't get a response**

    a. If you don't hear back within a week, follow up via email. If you don't hear back after another week, move to the phone.

    b. If you still don't get a response after 3-4 attempts (each a week apart), put the person on the back burner and move on to other contacts.

4. **Do additional research**

    a. Once you've set up your call or meeting, spend 20-30 minutes doing research on *Google, LinkedIn, Facebook*, and any other sources you have access to (e.g., *Bloomberg, FactSet, or Capital IQ*) and figure out where they went to school, where they've worked, and other details such as the deal types they've worked on.

    b. Don't go crazy with this; you just want enough information to properly frame your questions. Don't turn into a stalker and create 10-page bios of everyone.

5. **Make the call or attend the meeting**

    a. Aim for 10-15 minutes for a call and 30 minutes for a coffee meeting. Start by asking about their work and educational background and how they got to where they are today.

    b. Try to draw out their interests, hobbies, and anything notable they've done as opposed to asking generic questions like, "Where do you think the industry/economy is heading?" Be personal if you want to be remembered.

6. **Make your "mini-ask"**

a. As the conversation or meeting is drawing to a close, ask if it's OK to follow up with any additional questions you have, ask for referrals, if applicable, and suggest meeting in person in the future.

b. Why should you ask for favors in your first call or meeting?

c. To condition the person into helping you.

d. It's just like dating: if you treat someone as a friend, you will never move beyond the "friend zone." If you want a relationship, you need to act like more than a friend from the start. If you want to get interviews from your networking efforts, you need to ask for them.

7. **Follow-up**

   a. Aim for a follow-up every 2-3 months so they would remember you. Make sure the follow-up has a reason, referral, help with recruiting, and follow-up questions from the initial meeting.

8. **Make your "real ask"**

   a. "I hope all is well. With recruiting season approaching, I wanted to follow up and ask you how I could best position myself for an interview with your firm." You're not asking for an interview; you're asking how to "position yourself," for one.

   b. If you don't hear back, follow up once more via email and then move to the phone.

   c. Your goal is to get the other person to ask for your resume/CV and then receive a strong recommendation from that person at their firm. One final point: just because the other person "passed along" your resume/CV does not mean he/she actually did anything. Often, busy professionals say they'll help you but forget to do so, or they get too busy and never get around to it.

   d. So even after you send your resume/CV, you still need to follow up and ask about your status.

   e. "Relationship development" is an exhausting process, and it's not feasible to stay in touch with 500+ people consistently.

Other Avenues: Information Sessions and Weekend Trips

Those are the ABCs of how to conduct informational interviews, but you can always meet people elsewhere. As such, information sessions and weekend trips are viable options.

Information Sessions

Focus on people with the fewest number of wannabe bankers surrounding them.

Go up and make a joke about the news, the information session itself, or other people there to win their attention. Chat for a few minutes and focus on personal matters, travel, and hobbies/interests, and avoid "So, what's it like being an investment banker?"

If you get along "OK," but not spectacularly, make an excuse after 5-10 minutes and say you have to run, and then get their business card before you take off. Then, move on and repeat this process with everyone else in the room.

If you do hit it off really well, stay and chat and leverage the crap out of it; you might win an interview on the spot.

Afterward, quick follow-up is essential. Contact everyone who showed any interest in you within 1-2 days and ask for 10-15 minutes to speak on the phone or meet in person and request recruiting advice.

Weekend Trips

A weekend trip to New York, London, or whichever financial center is closest to you is an excellent way to get interviews, but only if you do it the right way.

Aim for 5-10 meetings each day, split between morning and afternoon, and make sure each "block" of meetings is in the same area of the city, so you're not running around constantly.

Plan for each meeting to last 30 minutes, and request everything 2-3 weeks in advance of your trip. Then, follow up right before the trip to confirm.

During the weekend of your trip, make sure you have a "reserve" list of people you can contact in case any meetings are canceled (50%+ will be canceled due to work emergencies) and that you have all the necessary phone numbers, email addresses, and bios with you.

The goal of a weekend trip is to meet as many people as possible near their offices and then get invited INTO the office to meet everyone else there.

Cold-Calling/Emailing

Cold-calling is even simpler than "developing relationships" because you don't need to develop a relationship; you just need to call boutique banks (or other small finance firms) repeatedly and ask for a job. This requires persistence on your part.

Here are the steps:

1. **Perfect your pitch**

    a. See the "Abbreviated Story" samples above. Your "pitch" for a cold call is just a 1-2 sentence version of your story, plus a request for an interview at the end.

    b. Here's a template you could use:

        i. "Hi [Person Name], my name is (Your Name), and I am (Student at University Name/Analyst at Firm Name, etc.). I wanted to get some information from you about how best to secure a (Name the Position) position at (Bank Name). Is now a good time to speak?"

        ii. Even though this is short, you are likely to stumble and stutter unless you practice a few times first. Try it in front of the mirror, and then practice "for real" by cold-calling companies in a different region or banks you don't care about as much.

2. **Make your list**

    a. Focus on local and boutique firms; in most cases, it's a waste of time to cold-call people at large banks. If you happen to get their contact information somehow, sure, go ahead and call, but focus on the smaller places.

3. **Refine your list**

    a. It's better to get bankers' contact information, but if you can't find it, settle for the main line, look up banker bios on the website, and ask to speak with a specific person when you call.

    b. Before calling, verify that everything is up-to-date and that all the banks and people still exist.

4. **Place your calls**

a. Now start placing your calls—aim for 5-10 minutes at most with each one. If you get the main line, ask for a banker by name. If you get sent to voicemail, hang up, call the secretary back, say you got disconnected, and ask for the banker's direct line or cell number.

b. Do not take "no" for an answer until you speak with someone who makes recruiting decisions. Answer any negative comment with: "So, you're in charge of recruiting there?" and when they say "No" or "Well..." ask to speak with whoever is in charge.

5. **Follow-up**

a. Follow up every 3-5 business days with each firm until you receive a definitive "yes" or "no" response. Even if they say "no," still follow up every few weeks to remind them who you are and see if anything has changed.

b. If they've said "no" to you consistently over several months, then it's time to move on and stop bothering with them.

6. **Rinse, wash, and repeat**

a. Once you get the basic process down, repeat it until you win interviews and offers. If you run out of local firms to contact, expand your scope and travel to other cities in your state or country that have more opportunities.

b. More so than "relationship development," cold-calling truly is 99% perspiration and 1% inspiration.

c. It's like hitting on people randomly in a bar: most of them will say "no" immediately, but eventually, someone will cave in and say "yes" (or at least "maybe").

Sample Relationship Development Process and Timeline

Here's a sample timeline you might follow if you're in school right now and you're looking for a summer internship next year:

- July: Begin making your list and contacting people.
- August: Continue to get referrals and focus on the most helpful contacts.

- September: Move to in-person informational interviews and think about weekend trips.
- October: Plan for your first weekend trip early in the fall.
- November: Follow up with everyone you've met, and plan for your 2nd-weekend trip to occur just before recruiting starts.
- December: During your second weekend trip, make sure you're on the "interview list" everywhere.
- January—February: As you move through interviews, continue networking and setting up in-person meetings.
- March and Beyond: If you don't already have an offer, don't give up; just shift your focus to boutiques and smaller firms, cold-calling where necessary.

The entire networking process is 99% perspiration and 1% inspiration

By following the guidelines above, you'll be ahead of 90% of prospective bankers when it comes to networking.

The Resume and CV That Gets You Interviews

Once you begin contacting bankers, you'll be asked for your resume or CV, so you need to be prepared with a document that will win your interviews and offers.

One Page Only

Unless you're more senior and you have extensive transaction experience, your resume should be 1 page. The only exception is in Australia, where 2-4 page resumes are more common.

The Rule of 3

No matter how much experience you have, you can't list everything. Focus on the 2-4 key full-time jobs, internships, or activities where you held a leadership role.

Bankers work 70-80+ hours per week and review hundreds of resumes, so they will not remember or care about all 27 different student groups you were in.

Project-Centric vs. Task-Centric

For each entry, use either a project-centric or task-centric structure. Start with a summary sentence giving your overall results, and then go into specific projects, clients, deals, or tasks you completed.

Project-centric structures are the best for consulting, investment banking, private equity, hedge funds, law, accounting, finance, and other "professional" fields, while task-centric structures are better for everything else.

Specifics and Results

Within each bullet, give the specifics of what you did, followed by the results, including numbers:

"Developed new social media marketing campaign for a TV network client; led to 20% rating growth in the new series lineup".

"Valued client using DCF and public company comparables; resulted in a valuation 10% higher than management's expectations".

Shouldn't This Be Harder?

I've purposely kept the resume section brief because it's mostly about using the right template and picking the right experience.

You should not overthink your resume if you're a university student applying for internships because your networking efforts and interview skills matter far more.

Once you've had substantial work experience, it gets trickier to craft a great resume because you have to be more selective with the experiences and language you use.

Cover Letters

The cover letters should only be four paragraphs long at most and less than one page long. It should follow the below structure;**are** any deviations from that writing too much and providing irrelevant information.

The Information at the Top

Nothing too fancy here. Your name and contact information could go on the right side, while the recruiter's/firm's name and contact information could go on the left.

If you don't have a name, don't panic—just use the company name and address instead. Yes, it's better to have a real name and send it to a real person, but it's not a deal breaker.

Similarly, "Dear so-and-so" works better if "so-and-so" is someone's name, but if you don't have it, "Dear Sir or Madam" is acceptable.

Paragraph 1: Introduction

Here's where you say who you are and how you learned about the opportunity—from networking, from an event, from a friend, or however else you found out. Then, you say what attracts you to the company and the specific position.

Keep this short; 2 to 3 sentences are best.

Paragraph 2: Your Background

This is usually your longest paragraph. Start out by writing what you're currently doing and then give the relevant internships/jobs you've had. Focus on useful skills (e.g., financial analysis) and whatever you did that's applicable to banking, trading, or whatever you're applying for.

A reverse chronological structure works well because, most of the time, your most relevant experience will also be the most recent.

I would use no more than five sentences for this one.

Paragraph 3: Why You're a Good Fit

This is a shorter paragraph. You should explain why your skills/experiences match whatever you're applying for and re-iterate what makes you interested.

If you have anything unique (for example, you're applying to a middle-market private equity firm after having run your own middle-market company), you may also want to mention it here as another selling point.

Paragraph 4: Conclusion

Remind them that your resume is enclosed, give your contact information and say that you look forward to hearing from them soon. Keep this to a few short sentences.

Behavioral and Qualitative Questions and Answers

Personal/Resume Q and A

These questions are /generally free for all and "go through your resume" type of questions. This portion of the question generally starts at the beginning of the interview and sets a tone for the rest of the interview.

This is also where you can pitch your story and how your experience and background have helped prepare you for a job in Investment Banking.

1. Walk me through your resume.

Start at "the beginning"—if you're in college, that might be where you grew up or where you went to high school. For anyone in business school or beyond, it might be where you went to undergraduate, your first job, or even where you went to business school. Then, go through how you first became interested in finance/business, how your interest developed over the years via the specific internships/jobs/other experiences you had, and conclude with a strong statement about why you're interviewing today.

Aim for 2-3 minutes—no longer than this, and the interviewer may become bored or impatient. Also, do not look at your resume when going through your "story."

The four most important points:

1. Be chronological.
2. Show how each experience along the way led you in the direction of finance
3. State why you're here interviewing today.
4. Aim for 2-3 minutes.

What are the most common mistakes with the "Walk me through your resume" question?

1. Going out of order chronologically.
2. Too much exposition—don't start off by saying, "I've had a lot of great experiences."

3. Being too short (under 1 minute) or too long (over 5 minutes).
4. Not sounding certain you want to do banking/finance.
5. Listing your experiences rather than giving a logical transition between each one.

2. Why did you major in (Your Major)?

If it was something related to business/economics, you could discuss your interest in those fields; for other majors, you can emphasize how you liked the challenge and/or had a personal interest in the field but also took the time to learn the basics of business/finance on your own.

3. What was your favorite class in college/business school?

I would not say anything economics/finance-related; it sounds too artificial. Tell them about something you were actually interested in—even if it's not directly related to banking. They want to see who you are as a person, not whether or not you know all the Excel shortcuts in the book, they probably ask you that later.

4. Why did you attend (Your University/Business School)? I'm sure you had many options/Why did you transfer to (University Name)?

Say that you looked at a lot of places but settled on wherever you went due to its excellent academic reputation, its strong business/finance/economics program, or something of that nature. If you were interested in something specific, it offered (e.g. you were an athlete and went to Stanford on scholarship, or you went to UChicago because of its excellent liberal arts program), you can mention that as well. Try to sound like you made a thoughtful decision rather than deciding randomly.

If you transferred elsewhere, a similar strategy applies, but make sure to emphasize it was for academic reasons. For example, don't say you wanted to get out of Massachusetts and move to southern California for an "improved lifestyle!"

5. What do you do for fun?

Obviously, don't say anything illegal or questionable/controversial. If you have anything interesting or not very common (hang gliding, directing movies, bungee-jumping), you should bring that up. Otherwise, just be honest , and if you really like watching football (North American football for international readers) or other sports, just talk about your interest in those.

6. What are your favorite movies or books?

There are two common mistakes:

1. Saying something like Wall Street, American Psycho, or Liar's Poker indicates you're a boring person.

2. Saying something like Harry Potter that indicates you're borderline illiterate.

Pick something in the middle—above pop literature/film but not something that has to do with finance specifically. That just sounds weird.

7. I see you wrote here that you're fluent in (Language). Can you tell me about your most recent internship in (Language)?

Be prepared for this if you list any common languages on your resume (Spanish, French, Italian, German, Chinese, Japanese, etc.) or if you happen to "get lucky" and your interviewer is a native speaker in one of the languages you've listed. I would suggest some practice discussing your work experience in whatever language(s) you've listed and making sure you can speak intelligently, at least briefly, about what you've done.

If you really don't know much, just tell them upfront rather than making a fool of yourself and trying to talk about EBITDA when you don't know the word for it; I speak from experience on this one.

Analytical or Attentions to Details Q and A

Very similar to the personal Q&A, you need to come up with stories and annotations that would explain why you are analytical and have good attention to detail. The interviewer is trying to assess whether you are comfortable with numbers and data and are not looking for a math whiz.

A lot of liberal arts students struggle with these questions because they neither have any quantitative classes nor work experience. Again, the interviewer is not looking for a math whiz, so any analytical example, such as from your day-to-day life, can be used. For example, a liberal arts major who lists poker as a hobby took us through his thought process on how he played one of his hands.

If you have not majored in something quantitative, expect more of these analytical or "comfortable with numbers" kinds of questions. This goes vice versa for graduates with quantitative backgrounds.

8. I see you've done mostly journalism and research internships before. Can you discuss your quantitative skills?

You should respond by discussing specific times when you had to analyze numbers and/or use logic. Good examples might include your personal portfolio, any math/science classes you've taken, any hobbies that require numbers, any type of budgeting processes you've been through, and any type of research you've done that involved numbers.

9. In your last internship, you analyzed portfolios and recommended investments to clients. Can you walk me through your thought process for analyzing the returns of a client portfolio?

The key is to break everything down into steps and be very specific about what you did. So you might say that "Step 1" was getting a list of when they bought each investment and how much they invested or how many shares they acquired; "Step 2" was finding a list of when they sold each investment and what they sold them for; and "Step 3" was aggregating this data over the years in between for each investment to calculate the compound return.

10. You were an English major—how do you know you can handle the quantitative rigor required in investment banking?

Combine the answers to questions #8 for this one. The key is to use specific examples rather than just saying, "I got a high math SAT score!" Personal financial experiences, classes, self-study courses, and independent study work well.

11. You've been working as a lawyer for the past 3 years—what initiative have you taken on your own to learn more about finance?

You should either present a list of self-study courses or certifications, such as the CFA that you've obtained, or speak about your own work, studying independently from textbooks, self-study courses, and other sources. Be conservative with how much you claim to know—re-iterate that you're "not an expert" but that you have taken the initiative to learn something on your own.

12. Can you tell me about a time when you submitted a report or project with misspellings or grammatical mistakes?

It's unrealistic to claim that you're perfect and have never done this. Instead, briefly mention a time when you made a careless mistake and then spend the majority of time in your answer discussing what you learned and how you improved, citing another specific example of how you improved the second time around.

13. How well can you multi-task?

In keeping with our theme of specificity, give a concrete example of a time when you were working on multiple projects at the same time—work, school, or activities work equally well for this one. Also, emphasize that despite the considerable demands, you pulled off everything successfully. Anything involving teamwork or collaboration is also good to use in this response.

Changing Careers Q and A

You probably haven't been thinking about being an investment banker since age 5. But if you've been in an unrelated industry for a while, you need to be well-prepared for "career change" questions. It's best to point to a specific anecdote or someone who sparked your initial interest in finance—assuming you have a story or person in mind.

14. You've had tons of engineering experience, and you've worked at many tech companies. Why do you want to be an investment banker now?

Talk about how you dislike the limited advancement opportunities and how your work didn't affect the world at large—only what that specific company was doing. You want to do finance because you like the business aspect of technology more than the technology aspect of technology and because you want to make an impact with your work and become an investor or advisor one day.

15. You've done Big 4 accounting for the past year—why would you want a job that's a lot more stressful with twice the hours?

You find accounting work boring and mundane because there are limited advancement opportunities. Finance is faster-paced, and you've realized that after speaking with a lot of friends and doing your own research, it's just more suited to your personality.

16. I see you worked at McKinsey one summer and then went to Citi investment banking the next year. Are you sure you want to do investment banking?

Yes. Although you worked at McKinsey, you realized you didn't like consulting because of the wishy-washy nature of the work (making reports and billing by the hour rather than billing by the result) and the constant travel and lack of quantitative skills or learning.

You enjoyed your Citi internship much more and realized you wanted to be in banking rather than consulting.

17. Wow. I must be honest; I rarely see people who have accomplished as much as you have at your age. You sold your own company for over $1 million within 2 years of starting it and became a leading real estate investor in Asia at the same time. Why would you ever want to work for other people in banking if you've been so successful on your own?

You don't view things in those terms. Although you did well, there's always room to learn, and banking would be a great learning opportunity for you. You've spoken with many friends in the industry and have been impressed by what you've heard, and you want to broaden your experience and knowledge so that you can move into a higher-stakes business.

18. You've worked at a few prop trading firms and also in Sales and Trading. They get paid pretty well and work market hours—so they have it a lot better than us. Why would you want to switch to investment banking?

You didn't like the culture of trading and wanted to have more of an impact by advising companies on major strategic decisions rather than just making small trades and investments each day. Banking excites you more because of the broader range of opportunities and experiences it gives you.

Culture Q andA

I never heard a good answer to the "Why our firm?" question in an interview, but that doesn't mean you can't try.

To do so, focus on the people—whom you've met and spoken with there, what they've told you about the firm, and what appeals to you.

Most banks have very similar cultures; people are nice but competitive and driven, and there's the expectation that you can do endless amounts of work for the firm.

And that's why focusing on people and anecdotes works much better than giving generic answers.

Other variants of this question include why you want to move to a larger or smaller firm. You can get away with more generic responses in those cases, but if you have a good story, you should definitely bring it up.

19. You spent this last summer working at Morgan Stanley's investment banking division. It seems like you'd be crazy not to go back. Why would you want to work for a smaller firm in our M&A group?

You're most likely to get this one if you didn't get a return offer—let's be honest, who really goes from Morgan Stanley to a boutique? It's a tough sell, but you'll have to emphasize how you like the smaller environment where you get more responsibility and work more closely with clients. The banker probably won't believe you, but it's better than outright admitting you didn't get an offer.

If the topic does arise, just say your lack of offer was because they were not hiring, because the group did poorly, or because of the general economic climate.

20. Since you worked at Bank of America this past year, you probably have the chance to go to a lot of different large banks. Why are you interested in us specifically?

There's rarely a "great" way to answer this question, so I would recommend either referencing someone you've spoken with at the bank and what they've told you or if you don't have any kind of experience like that, you can just give the usual generic reasons given for each bank. This question often reflects a lazy interviewer more than anything else; the real reason you're interviewing with any bank is because they've given you an interview!

21. When you were working at that boutique this past summer, you mentioned how you liked the smaller team and more hands-on environment. Why not just go back there? Why do you want to move to a large bank?

It's always good to be positive about your experience, but at the same time, you also want to give a good reason as to why you're moving elsewhere. If you're moving from a smaller bank to a larger one, you want to emphasize learning about how larger/major deals happen, how you want to learn from the best, and perhaps even how bankers at your old firm recommended that you go somewhere bigger at the beginning of your career.

22. Why are you interested in our M or A division rather than our industry groups? Our Tech, Healthcare, and Energy teams have been really successful this year.

Say that you want to gain solid technical and modeling skills and be exposed to a wide variety of industries and different markets. Depending on the interviewer, it may also be appropriate to mention your interest in private equity (if you're planning to go that route) and how M and A will get you there.

M and A bankers love to think they're superior to others because of their "in-depth technical knowledge and negotiation skills," so you should play off that and use it to your advantage.

23. Why do you want to work in Capital Markets? There's hardly any market activity these days.

With this type of question—whenever a certain area is depressed at the moment or is not doing well—you want to highlight your long-term view of the market and how things recover over time.

For Capital Markets specifically, you can talk about your interest in the markets since you were much younger and how you've always been fascinated by IPOs, secondary offerings, and such—as always, specific examples are the key to success.

Career Goals Q and A

Career goals and future aspirations need to be crafted with your current career level in mind. If you are interviewing for any positions higher than an analyst, you have to show that you have your mind set on investment banking for the long term and make sure not to even hint that you are pursuing anything else.

When you are an Analyst, it is known that you have not actually been through the rounds yet, so it is not 100% certain that you see yourself as an investment banker in the future. At the same time, you don't want to veer too far away from business or finance.

24. I realize it's still early in your career—you haven't even graduated yet, but have you given any thought to your long-term plans? Do you think you'll stick with investment banking?

If you're interviewing for an Analyst position, you can be more uncertain about your future and just state you don't know 100% where you'll be yet, but banking is what excites you most and is what will give you the skills you need to succeed. For prospective associates, you need to be more certain about your career path and show some commitment. Indicate that you've done your homework, spoken with many people, and really want to make a career out of it.

25. You've had quite diverse experience prior to business school. After you complete your degree, where do you think you'll be going in the long term?

Since this question is given to an MBA candidate, you'll want to be more certain and show more direction in terms of your plans. State that you do want to pursue investment banking as a career after having done extensive research on your own (and hopefully, having had a previous internship or other experience in the field that you can point to).

26. What is your career goal?

This might be my least favorite question of all time, but some lazy interviewers will ask you, anyway. Again, at the undergraduate level, you can afford to be more vague and just indicate you want to do something in business/finance and advance to a high level; MBA candidates should indicate that they're in banking for the long term.

27. Looking into the future 10 years, do you think you'll still be an investment banker?

Analysts can, and arguably should, be more uncertain, while business school graduates need to be confident about their career choices.

Strength and Weakness Q and A

You're not likely to get the standard "Tell me your strengths and weaknesses" question in investment banking interviews; a more plausible variant is "Tell me the feedback you received in your most recent internship or job." The most common mistake? Not actually giving strengths and weaknesses.

This might sound crazy, but I've conducted many interviews and have seen this one countless times.

You need to focus on the qualities bankers look for when listing your strengths and give a brief example to back up what you say if you mention something like "attention to detail" or "hardworking."

When giving weaknesses, make sure you list a real, but not critical, weakness. Don't say your weakness is that you "work too hard," but also don't say that your weakness is your "inability to get work done on time." Something like "being too critical of others" or "getting lost in the details" works better.

You also need to include something about how you have improved upon your weaknesses and/or overcome failures in the past.

28. In your internship this past summer, what feedback did you receive?

This is a variant of the "strengths and weaknesses" question. The most common mistake is being vague and just saying you performed well and they liked you and then failing to give weaknesses or areas for improvement.

The right way to answer this question is to state specific qualities about you that they liked—such as ambition, drive, attention to detail, or willingness to go the extra mile for the team—and then give some specific examples of times when you demonstrated those qualities. Your all-nighters, the times you stayed the weekend working on a presentation, or the times you caught mistakes someone else above you missed are all good to mention.—

The other critical part is to mention weaknesses or areas for improvement as well—talk about real weaknesses and how you've worked to improve them (see more on this in #2 below).

29. What were a few areas that your team said you should try to improve upon?

The two most important points to remember with the "weaknesses" or "failure" question:

1. Give a real weakness rather than saying you "work too hard."
2. Show how you improved on it, using specific examples.

What are "real" weaknesses you could give? Maybe you weren't as communicative with the team as you should have been at the start; maybe you got lost in the details sometimes and failed to see the big picture; maybe you were too impatient with others or did not delegate tasks appropriately.

The point is to say something that is a real weakness but which is also not a "deal breaker"—like saying you don't like to work hard or can't stand working in teams. After that, state how you're working to improve your weaknesses. Perhaps you gave more regular updates to your superiors, or maybe you started leveraging other people's knowledge or the administrative staff at your work more often.

30. Did you get an offer to return to where you worked last summer?

If you did get an offer, this is an easy question: "Yes." If you did not receive an offer, I would strongly recommend against lying about it; state that you did not receive an offer, and it was due to the economy, because your group was not hiring, or due to other forces beyond your control.

The danger with lying is that finance is a very small world, and it's quite easy to ask a friend or a friend of a friend what really happened.

31. Let's imagine that your best friend is describing you in 3 words. Which words would he/she use and why?

This is just "Tell me your strengths" in disguise, but you need to narrow it down to 3 words. Since it's your friend describing you, you don't want to say, "Driven, attentive to detail, and a team player!"

You do want to convey the same ideas—that you can work hard, play well in teams, and get things done no matter what obstacles you face—but you should pick your own language to get this across.

For each word you list, you should also give 1-2 sentences to back up what you say, using a specific example for each one.

32. Imagine that I'm speaking to someone with whom you have not gotten along in the past. What would he/she say about you?

This is just a disguised "weaknesses" question. However, since it involves someone else this time, it's better to give a weakness, such as being stubborn and holding too rigidly to your own views, rather than some of the other faults you could state. Weaknesses related to team/group settings are better here.

And once again, you need to emphasize how you've worked to improve whatever it is that you did not do well at the time.

Don't say something like, "I get along with everyone!" as that sounds unrealistic.

32. Why would we decide not to give you an offer today?

This one is a bit tricky because it's so direct. You could attempt to make a joke out of this one and say something like, "If you decided you weren't hiring at all!" but that may not go well if your interviewer doesn't appreciate the humor.

Otherwise, the best response may be to turn this around and say, "I see no reason why you wouldn't. I'm your best choice because...." and then give your strengths instead. If they really press you on this, you can admit a weakness and then say how you've been working to improve it.

33. Tell me why we should hire you in three sentences.

This is yet another variation of the "strengths" question. But rather than giving generic strengths, you should highlight any unique experiences you've had. So maybe you haven't had banking internships before, but you have had unique experience abroad, in an unusual setting, or doing something, not many others have done, or you've overcome unusual hardship, and those make you particularly well-qualified.

Try to make your answer some variant of "I'm smart because of (school or academics), I can do the work because of (Internships or Previous jobs), and I'm an interesting person and fun to be around because of [unique experience]."

34. What was your greatest failure?

As with any "weaknesses" question, you need to use a specific story—such as an exam in which you did not do well, a project that did not go as planned, or a work situation that did not turn out well and show what you learned from it and how you've improved since then. Don't say something fake like, "My greatest failure was getting into Yale and Princeton but not Harvard"—that makes you look silly. It's better to give something real and then show how you've used the failure to develop.

Understanding Banking Q and A

Are you sure you understand investment banking? Are you really sure? Most people going through the interview process—whether students, professionals, or MBAs—have no idea what they're getting into.

The "Understanding Banking" questions are designed to separate the wheat from the chaff—to verify that you have done your homework and are prepared to accept 80-100 hours per week.

You're more likely to get these questions if you're a career changer or you've never had a banking internship before.

Fortunately, they are relatively easy to answer as long as you've done some research and know the basics.

35. You've never worked in finance before. How much do you know about what bankers actually do?

You should acknowledge that although you haven't worked in the field before, you've done a lot of research on your own and have spoken with many friends in the industry.

Based on that, you know that bankers advise companies on transactions—buying and selling other companies and raising capital. They are "agents" that connect a company with the appropriate buyer, seller, or investor.

The day-to-day work involves creating presentations, financial analysis, and marketing materials, such as executive summaries.

36. Let's say I'm working on an IPO for a client. Can you describe briefly what I would do?

First, you meet with the client and gather basic information, such as their financial details, an industry overview, and who their customers are.

Next, you meet with other bankers and lawyers to draft the S-1 registration statement, which describes the company's business and markets it to investors. You receive some comments from the SEC and keep revising the document until it's acceptable.

Then, you spend a few weeks going on a "road show" where you present the company to institutional investors and convince them to invest. Afterward, the company begins trading on an exchange once you've raised the capital from investors.

37. Can you tell me about the different product and industry groups at our bank?

This one is bank-dependent and will differ for boutiques, middle-market firms, and bulge brackets; therefore, you need to research it before your interview. Typical product groups include Mergers and Acquisitions (M&A), Leveraged Finance (LevFin), and

Restructuring; you could also consider Equity Capital Markets and Debt Capital Markets "product groups," but that one is debatable.

Common industry groups include Healthcare, Retail, Industrials, Energy, Natural Resources, Financial Institutions, Gaming, Real Estate and Technology, Media and Telecom (TMT).

Not all banks are structured this way; for example, Goldman Sachs does not have product groups and instead handles all types of deals in its industry groups.

Meanwhile, most bulge-bracket banks do not have restructuring groups at all, which is something that only middle-market and boutique firms do.

Finally, a lot of boutiques focus only on M and A and/or restructuring, and ones that are small enough are not even split into industry groups.

38. What's in a pitch book?

It depends on the type of deal the bank is pitching for, but the most common structure is:

1. Bank "credentials" (similar deals they've done to "prove" their expertise).
2. Summary of a company's options ("strategic alternatives" in banker-speak).
3. Valuation and appropriate financial models (for example, if you're pitching for an IPO, you might show where the IPO proceeds would go).
4. Potential acquisition targets (buy-side M and A deal) or potential buyers (sell-side M and A deal). This is not applicable to equity/debt deals.
5. Summary and key recommendations.

38. How do companies select the bankers they work with?

This is usually based on relationships; banks develop relationships with companies over the years before they need anything, and then when it comes time to do a deal, the company calls different banks it has spoken with and asks them to "pitch" for the business. This is called a "bake-off," and the company selects the "winner" afterward.

39. Walk me through the process of a typical sell-side M and A deal.

A typical sell-side M and A deal with many potential buyers would look like this:

1. Meet with a company, create initial marketing materials like the Executive Summary and Offering Memorandum (OM), and decide on potential buyers.

2. Send out an Executive Summary to potential buyers to gauge interest.

3. Send NDAs (Non-Disclosure Agreements) to interested buyers along with more detailed information like the Offering Memorandum, and respond to any follow-up due diligence requests from the buyers.

4. Set a "bid deadline" and solicit written Indications of Interest (IOIs) from buyers.

5. Select which buyers advance to the next round.

6. Continue responding to information requests and setting up due diligence meetings between the company and potential buyers.

7. Set another bid deadline and pick the "winner."

8. Negotiate terms of the Purchase Agreement with the winner and announce the deal.

40. Walk me through the process of a typical buy-side M and A deal.

1. Spend a lot of time upfront doing research on dozens or hundreds of potential acquisition targets, and go through multiple cycles of selection and filtering with the company you're representing.

2. Narrow down the list based on their feedback and decide which ones to approach.

3. Conduct meetings and gauge the receptivity of each potential seller.

4. As discussions with the most likely seller become more serious, conduct more in-depth due diligence and figure out your offer price.

5. Negotiate the price and key terms of the Purchase Agreement and then announce the transaction.

41. Walk me through a debt issuance deal.

1. It's similar to the IPO process:

2. Meet with the client and gather basic financial, industry, and customer information.

3. Work closely with DCM/Leveraged Finance to develop a debt financing or LBO model for the company and figure out what kind of leverage, coverage ratios and covenants might be appropriate.

4. Create an investor memorandum describing all of this.

5. Go out to potential debt investors and win commitments from them to finance the deal.

The main differences vs. an IPO: there are fewer banks involved, and you don't need SEC approval to do any of this because debt is not sold to the "general public" but rather to sophisticated institutional investors and funds.

42. How are Equity Capital Markets (ECM) and Debt Capital Markets (DCM) different from M and A or industry groups?

ECM and DCM are both more "market-based" than M and A. In M and A, your job is to execute sell-side and buy-side transactions, whereas in ECM or DCM, most of your tasks are related to staying on top of the market, following current trends, and making recommendations to industry and product groups for clients and pitch books.

In ECM/DCM, you go more in-depth on certain parts of the deal process, but you don't get as broad a view as you might in other groups.

43. What's the difference between DCM and Leveraged Finance?

They're similar, but Leveraged Finance is more "modeling-intensive" and does more of the deal execution with industry and M and A groups on LBOs and debt financings. DCM, by contrast, is more closely tied to the markets and tracks trends and relevant data.

But there's always overlap, and some banks have just 1 of these groups, some have both, and some divide it differently altogether.

44. Explain what a divestiture is?

It's when a company (public or private) decides to sell off a specific division rather than sell the entire company. The process is very similar to the sell-side M and A process above, but it tends to be "messier" because you're dealing with a part of one company rather than the whole thing.

Creating a "standalone operating model" for the particular division they're selling is extremely important, and the transaction structure and valuation are more complex than they would be for a "plain-vanilla" M and A deal.

45. Imagine you want to draft a 1-slide company profile for an investor. What would you put there?

"Put the name of the company in the header, then divide the slide into four equal parts. The top left is for the business description, headquarters, and key executives. Put a stock chart and the key historical and projected financial metrics and multiples on the top right. The bottom left can have descriptions of products and services, and the bottom right should have key geographies with a color-coded map to make it look pretty."

"The Market" Q and A

"The Market" questions are designed to test your sense of business, economics, and investing. Even though you won't be investing as an investment banker, you still must look at a business and tell what's appealing about it and what might be cause for concern.

Common questions include how you would invest a large sum of money, how you would think about investing in companies, and how you would decide whether to start a business of your own.

You could also get more general questions about recent industry trends, companies you follow that are particularly interesting, and anything you've personally invested in.

To answer these questions successfully, you need to ask the right questions before giving an answer. Which questions, specifically?

1. Always ask what the investor or business goals are.
2. Always ask if there are any constraints, limitations, time horizons, or any other limiting factors.

You should also be citing specific numbers and figures where applicable.

These types of questions often turn into extended dialogues where you try to convince the interviewer of the merits of a particular company or investment.

46. Let's say you had $10 million to invest in anything. What would you do with it?

Always ask for the investor's goals first. Are they looking to have big capital gains over 30-40 years? Are they looking for tax-free retirement income? What types of assets interest them?

Based on the response, you can give an appropriate answer. So if they're investing over 30-40 years and going for high capital gains, a well-diversified portfolio is probably best; if they are more concerned with tax-free income, maybe you should tell them about municipal bonds.

47. If you owned a small business and were approached by a larger company about an acquisition, how would you think about the offer, and how would you make a decision on what to do?

The key terms to consider would be:

1. Price
2. Forms of payment: cash, stock, or debt
3. Future plans for the company vis-à-vis your own plans.

Of course, there is much more to an M and A deal than this; you could list literally hundreds of different terms.

But those are the key ones. To make a decision, you'd have to weigh each one; there's no "magical" way to decide. You might also point out that if something is particularly important to you—such as retaining a role in the company—then a difference of intentions could be a "deal-breaker."

48. We do most of our work with technology companies. Can you talk about a trend or company in the industry that has piqued your interest lately?

This is very common if you're interviewing for any industry group. I recommend doing some research beforehand and being able to speak about trends in that market.

It's easy to find this information for technology and anything that sells to consumers, but it's a bit harder for something like chemicals.

Most interviewees make three mistakes with this question:

1. They describe something that is not recent or relevant. Don't talk about the emergence of the Internet; talk about how companies are shifting their software to the Internet.

2. They don't explain the "why"; they're shifting to the web because it's cheaper and lower maintenance for them.

3. They don't explain the impact on the market as a whole; such companies are growing very quickly while more traditional companies are either struggling or shifting to that model.

49. Let's say you could start any type of business you wanted, and you had $1 million in initial funds. What would you do?

You'll want to ask follow-up questions to see if the interviewer is looking for something more specific because this one is wide open.

If no further direction is provided, you probably want to say that you'd think about some type of niche business with high margins that requires little startup capital ($1 million is not enough to build 10 factories) and ongoing maintenance; those make it harder to turn a profit and sell the business one day.

(This is one reason why some private equity investors focus on software companies).

It's better to focus on a niche market because most broad, horizontal markets are already dominated by major companies (Microsoft, Goldman Sachs, Exxon Mobil, etc.).

You should also explain your reasoning on why this type of business would be attractive and how it could grow with minimal future investment.

50. Can you talk about a company you admire and what makes them attractive to you?

Do not say something commonly known. Saying *Google* or *Apple*, for example, would be bad. Instead, go more obscure and pick a company no one knows so that they can tell you've done your research and so that they're less likely to ask probing questions.

You don't necessarily need to give financial details, but if the company is public and you can easily find the information, it definitely helps.

When you talk about what makes the firm attractive, emphasize qualities that investors would find appealing, such as a great and well-diversified customer base, a unique competitive advantage in the market, or a high-margin business model. Don't say that you like them because your new iPhone is awesome.

51. Let's assume you are going to start a laundry machine business. How would you analyze whether it's viable?

To assess whether it's "viable," you have to determine whether you can make a profit with the business. For a laundry machine operation, you'd start by looking at the location (the most important part of any retail business), estimate how many customers you could get, how frequently they do laundry, and how much they pay each time to do their laundry. Those variables give you an idea of monthly or annual revenue.

On the expense side, the biggest cost would be the upfront construction and/or purchase of the building and the machinery. You would probably need a loan for this unless you had a spare $500K in your bank account.

You would also have to take into account the cost of maintaining and servicing the machines, building maintenance, and hiring someone to collect cash, clean, and open/close the building each day.

Overall, location plays the biggest role in the success of this type of business. If you put your new company next to an apartment complex where everyone has laundry machines, you're doomed from the beginning.

Incidentally, laundry machines happen to be very profitable businesses if run correctly, mostly because they are not labor intensive and do not require huge investments after you've gotten started. So you could even use this as an example for the "What kind of business would you start with $1 million?" question.

52. Tell me about an M and A deal that interested you recently.

You want to say who the buyer and seller were, and include background information if they are not household names—as well as the price and the multiples (Purchase Price/Revenue, Purchase Price/EBITDA) if they are readily available.

Read the relevant Wall Street Journal article on it, and discuss the dynamics of the deal: how it developed, whether anyone else was interested, and what implications it has for the industry.

You don't need to be an expert, but you do need to sound intelligent and know the basics. If they start asking for information you don't know, just admit upfront that you don't know whatever they've asked for.

53. Pitch me a stock

You can refer to #5 in this section—the company you admire—because both these questions are quite similar. One difference is that if the question is "pitch me a stock," you need to mention specific financial figures. Since the company is public, it shouldn't be too hard to find those.

Even if you can't get Revenue or EBITDA multiples, looking up its P/E multiple and saying whether it's higher or lower than competitors is a step in the right direction.

The two most common mistakes:

1. Failing to list specific financial figures.
2. Saying how the company stacks up relative to its competition and why its prospects are more favorable.

Structure your answer with the following five points in mind:

1. Give the name and summarize what the company does.
2. Give a brief overview of its financials to indicate its size and how profitable it is.
3. State how it's undervalued or more attractive than its rivals due to any competitive advantages it has.
4. Say how there is a long-term trend in its favor; it's not just looking good in the past month.
5. Talk about how the next 5-10 years will be really good for the company.

9. Can you explain to me, in simple terms, the subprime crisis?

In simple terms, banks made mortgage loans to people who were in no position to pay them off or even meet monthly payments. Since interest rates were at historical lows, borrowing was easy.

At the same time, mortgages were no longer just loans made to individuals; they were sliced up, combined, and "packaged" into securities that banks traded, acquired, and sold to investors.

A typical "package" might contain mortgages given to both "credible" borrowers as well as mortgages granted to more risky borrowers—the more risky ones were labeled "subprime."

Banks acquired these "packaged" assets on the argument that even if one "piece" of the asset was risky or likely to default, the rest still had value.

As it turns out, this was false, and no one knew what any of these mortgage-related assets were worth, but as unqualified homeowners began defaulting, buyers disappeared overnight, and the value of these assets plummeted to $0.

As a result, the value of many banks also approached $0, and quite a few failed or went bankrupt in the process—all because the securities were so complex that no one understood their value or the true risks involved.

54. Do you agree with the $700 billion bank bailout?

Your specific answer doesn't matter too much—just make sure you actually give an answer ("yes" or "no") and that you back it up with solid reasoning.

These days, it's probably better to say "yes" because, as we witnessed with the bankruptcy of Lehman Brothers, if a financial institution that's large enough collapses, it can have ripple effects and bring down the rest of the economy and financial markets along with it.

"Why Banking?" Q and A

After the "Walk me through your resume" question at the beginning of almost every interview, the "Why investment banking?" is the next most important question you'll get.

It is particularly important for the Career Changer, whether you're a working professional looking to get in, an MBA student who has worked in a different industry prior to business school, or a college student who hasn't had finance or business experience.

The two most important points to keep in mind:

1. You've done your homework and researched this thoroughly before jumping in. Cite specific people you've spoken with.

2. You have a long-term view of your career and are fine making a sacrifice in the short-term

55. I see you have no relevant finance experience. Why should we hire you over someone who's had a previous banking internship?

Talk about how banking is about what skills you bring to the table and what kind of person you are rather than how many internships you've had. Discuss how you've worked long hours, collaborated in teams,, and paid attention to details before and succeeded at whatever you've done.

If you're feeling bold, you can also point out that although someone might have had a banking internship, that doesn't mean he/she did well in it, and that you may be better equipped based on your own experience.

56. I see you've worked mostly in wealth management before. Why are you looking to switch to banking now?

You want to understand the bigger picture and how and why large companies make decisions rather than just working with individual investors. Working on transactions and making an impact is more interesting to you than giving individual advice to high-net-worth individuals (or institutions).

57. You're a smart guy/girl with a lot of options, and right now, the economy is not doing well, and lots of banks have failed. Why are you still interested in banking when you could do anything else?

Talk about your long-term view and how a downturn could be an even better time to enter the industry because you'll know how to work when times are both good and bad.

In addition, you've been interested in finance for a long time and are not going to let short-term difficulties deter you from entering the field; you've explored other options and concluded that this is the best one for you.

58. The economy has been improving lately, and more people are "getting interested" in finance. How do I know you're serious and not just following everyone else?

In theto reverse of question #3, you can apply a similar strategy here, but instead of discussing how it's an equally good time to start out in banking, just say that you hold a long-term view and haven't just become interested overnight. Being able to point to specific evidence of your interest, such as your own portfolio, the finance/business club you're in, or even day trading, also helps.

59. Where did your interest in finance begin?

Almost anything could work for this one—just make sure it's not too recent. Otherwise, it looks like you became interested in a whim.

Also, be sure to explain how your initial interest led you toVP level the internships, activities, or jobs you pursued and how those have led you to where you are today.

60. If you enjoyed your last internship and got an offer to come back. Why are you trying to switch to investment banking now?

You're looking for something faster-paced where there's a better learning opportunity and more of a chance to make an impact. You've also been interested all along and realize you really do want to do it now, after having explored other alternatives and not liked them.

If this is a small company to big company move (or vice versa), you can also say something about that, using the standard reasons we went through before—small means more responsibility and client interaction, and big means working on more major deals and learning more technical skills.

61. You've advanced into a high-paying position at your current company. Why would you want to move here, take a pay cut, and work twice the hours?

This is the key question asked of many career changers and anyone else at the VP level (or above) at a company who is looking to switch to banking as an associate.

Here are the major points to emphasize:

1. You've done your homework and spoken with a lot of people about this move, and you like the finance work you've done before.
2. Banking is faster-paced and appeals to you more because you make more of an impact.
3. You're fine with the pay cut and additional hours because of the improved opportunities to make an impact and advance.

Think Outside the Box Q and A

You're likely to receive a number of "outside the box" questions in interviews, especially if your interviewer is the creative type or if you've given "boring" answers in your interview so far.

The main mistake you can make here is taking yourself too seriously. With these questions, the interviewer is trying to get at what makes you "cool" and sets you apart from other people.

So try to have some fun with these.

62. What type of animal/vegetable would you be?

Some interviewees take this as a cue to tie your choice back to being a team player, hard worker, or such, but that's not the best approach.

For "creativity"-type questions, interviewers want you to be... creative. So think about your real personality and say something that matches that.

Example: Maybe you'd be a "hedgehog" because it looks like you have "spikes" on the outside to an observer, but you're actually warm and fuzzy on the inside.

63. Let's say that in the future your name turns up as the front page headline of a newspaper one day. What would the story be about?

With this type of question, you can show more "banker-like" traits such as ambition and hard work, but you shouldn't take it too seriously.

So maybe the headline states that you climbed Mt. Everest, sold your company in an IPO, or became a best-selling author; you want "ambition + creativity/coolness" for this type of question.

Hopefully, the headline wasn't about your indictment for insider trading.

64. Tell me a joke.

"Q: What was the best part of Playboy's IPO? A: The pitch book."

If you have a female interviewer or someone else who might get offended, then try the following corny but impossible-to-offend joke instead:

"A dog goes into an investment banking job interview, and the banker says to him, 'You've got the job, but only if you can do three things. First, you have to be able to complete an LBO model in 30 minutes.' So the dog runs to a computer and astoundingly creates a full model in 30 minutes.

"That's very nice! Next, you must be able to spread 10 comps manually in under an hour. Immediately, the dog sits down at the computer and completes everything in only 30 minutes. 'That's perfect! Lastly, you must be bilingual.' So then the dog says, 'Meow!' "

65. What's your personal Beta?

"Beta" in the Capital Asset Pricing Model (CAPM) measures expected return and expected risk. Higher Beta means a higher potential return but also more risk.

You probably want to say above 1.0, but not too much above it; you're much more ambitious than the average person, which causes you to try lots of new things and achieve quite a bit, so that inevitably carries some risk.

But you're not so reckless that you take careless risks; it's all about moderation. Don't go over 2.0.

Bankers like to think of themselves as "entrepreneurial" even though banking is extremely different from entrepreneurship, so you should take advantage of this line of thinking and indulge them.

66. What's the riskiest thing you've ever done?

Don't say "cocaine" or any other drug/porn-like/illegal activity. This should be common sense, but you wouldn't believe the emails I get.

But you also can't say, "I sat next to the unpopular kid one day..." because that's not risky at all. Try to discuss an internship or job experience you had that you never expected to get or some type of extracurricular/leadership experience that was somewhat random and turned out to be great and talk about how it was a calculated risk and that you got a lot out of the decision you made.

If you can point to something you had to be proactive to get, this is a good time to bring it up.

67. Let's say that you have $1 million, but you are NOT allowed to invest it or otherwise use it to create more money. What would you spend the capital on instead?

Don't say, "I would start my own business..." or "I would invest it in..."—many people completely ignore the actual question here.

It's best to tie this back to whatever your interests and passions, so you might use the money to support volunteer work you've done, extended travel that you've always wanted to take, or maybe even to buy that race car you've always wanted.

Just make sure your answer is believable—if you have never worked at a non-profit or in a volunteer group in your life, don't suddenly try to be a saint. If you love cars, say you would think about buying a car you've always wanted... among other things.

Deals Transaction and Mergers and Acquisitions Q and A

Having transaction experience is a blessing and a curse. It's great because you sound more credible in your interviews, but it's an added challenge because you need to know your stuff.

If you've worked on deals before, your interviewer will spend a lot of time asking you about what you did and will often "re-frame" the standard technical questions in the context of your deals instead.

The questions, explanations, and sample answers here focus on M and A deals because those are generally "better" to speak about in interviews, but you can tweak your answers and apply them to almost any kind of deal.

68. Walk me through one of the deals listed on your resume.

Try to pick an M and A deal rather than equity/debt financing and aim for more "unique" deal types like divestitures or distressed M and A; also try to pick something that's either "high-profile" or a deal where you contributed a lot.

Don't go into too much detail for an "opening question" like this; just give a brief overview and then let them ask the questions.

Describe the company, give approximate financial (revenue, EBITDA, market cap) figures, and say what they wanted to do.

Here's how you might describe a sell-side M and A deal you worked on:

"One of the deals I worked on was the sale of a $1 billion market cap consumer retail company. They specialized in food and beverages and sold to the US and European markets. Their revenue was around $800 million with $200 million EBITDA, growing at around 5% per year. They were interested in selling because of a string of recent acquisitions in their market and felt they could get a premium valuation. They engaged us to run a broad sell-side process with financial and strategic buyers."

Here's how you might describe an IPO:

"One deal I worked on was the $200 million IPO of a Chinese Internet company on the Hong Kong Stock Exchange. They had revenue of around $50 million, EBITDA of $10 million, and were growing very quickly, around 50% per year. They were going public to raise funds so that they could expand beyond China and get into other markets, and we were the lead underwriter on the deal."

After you finish your "introduction," the interviewer will start asking follow-up questions based on what you said.

69. Did you do anything quantitative for this deal? It looks like it just involved research.

This is a common scenario for summer interns or if you worked at a small boutique where financial modeling was not as common. Don't say that you did nothing quantitative, but also don't make it seem like you know everything there is to know about valuation or modeling. If you didn't build the model yourself, just point out how you contributed to it. Here's how you might respond:

"A lot of what I worked on was qualitative and involved researching potential buyers to see what the best fit might be. Our team did some valuation and financial modeling work as well, but since I was an intern, I supported the other Analyst and Associates by finding relevant facts and figures and then, going through their models, figuring out how they worked, and then making sure the information was correct."

70. Why did the company you were representing want to sell?

Maybe they received an unsolicited offer, maybe there had been a string of recent acquisitions in their market, maybe the founder wanted to exit the business, or maybe the PE firm that owned the company wanted to exit its investment. You might say something like the following:

They wanted to sell because larger companies in the market had recently acquired their closest competitors, and they felt that they could no longer thrive as a standalone entity.

Additionally, they had received informal offers from a few of the larger companies before and felt that the timing was right to explore a sale once again.

71. Why did the company you were representing want to buy another company?

For this one you need to talk about what specific type of other company they wanted to buy. Did they want to expand into new geographies? Get into a new industry? Pursue a "hot" start-up that was receiving a lot of attention? Here's an example:

"Our client was interested in expanding from midstream oil and gas production and wanted to get into the upstream market as well, especially in North America. They had tried to do so before, but lacked the expertise and industry contacts; so they wanted to acquire a sizable company that had already done it so they could grow their top line and also diversify their business."

72. Describe the deal process?

This one is completely dependent on what type of deal you worked on, but no matter what you say, don't go into an excruciating level of detail here. Focus on whether it was a broad or targeted process for M and A deals and what kinds of buyers/sellers you approached; for debt and equity financings, just go through the key points in the registration statements or investor memos and what the investor reaction was.

"We ran a broad sell-side auction process for our client. They had in mind around 10-20 strategic buyers that might have been interested, and we added around 30 financial sponsors to their list. We got serious interest from about 5 of the companies we approached, which led to 1 strategic buyer and one financial sponsor ultimately competing to win the deal."

73. What were the major selling points of your client? What was attractive about it?

This one applies for both sell-side deals and equity/debt financings—good points to raise might include financial performance, market and industry trends, any competitive advantages it enjoyed, and anything positive about its customer base. Stay away from talking about the strength of the management team because that is very difficult to "explain" in an interview.

"The Swedish healthcare company we were representing had been growing at around 15% year-over-year, vs. 5% average growth for the industry as a whole. It also had higher margins than other companies in the industry because it focused on high-end and more profitable medical care. The market as a whole was also very favorable because the Swedish population was aging, and demand for healthcare could only rise in years to come."

74. What about its weaknesses? Why might investors be hesitant?

You could talk about unfavorable market trends, increased competition, uncertain financial projections, or the threat of new regulation harming the company.

"Although our client had performed well in the European healthcare market, its financial projections depended on expanding into the US and Asia, and it had no track record there.

Also, massive healthcare reform in the US might make it significantly more difficult to enter that market in the future."

75. What were the major obstacles to getting the deal done? What happened?

These could be anything from disagreements on price to legal issues to problems with retaining the management team. If you can point to any obstacles that you played a role in resolving, bring them up here.

"We ran into issues because the private equity firm we were in discussions with wanted to make the deal contingent on the debt financing, which the CEO could not go along with. We also ran into problems with valuation because the PE firm discounted our projections by about 20%. Eventually, we compromised on both points and on the second issue. I helped create a more detailed revenue model for the company that validated some of our assumptions, so the PE firm agreed to meet us halfway."

76. What kind of standalone operating model did you create for your client?

For this one, you don't need to explain how to link the three statements together; focus on how you created the revenue model and the expense model. Usually, you do this by looking at revenue in terms of units sold, factories, or production, and you analyze expenses by fixed costs and employees.

"On the revenue side, we looked at our client's existing, proven oil reserves and used their historical exploration & production figures to project how much they would be adding each year vs. what would be depleted. Then, we combined that with projections for oil prices to estimate their yearly revenue. On the expense side, the majority of costs were tied to how many oil fields were operational, so we linked numbers for transportation, technology, and drilling costs to those."

77. What was the status of this deal when you left your bank?

Don't feel "pressured" to say that the deal closed or that the IPO was priced before you left. It's fine to say that it was still up in the air, and even if the deal actually fell apart, you're better off pretending that it's still pending and that there hasn't been an announcement yet (unless it was a huge deal that very publicly fell apart).

"When I left, both sides did not agree 100% on price. They were moving closer and had resolved management retention and had come to an agreement on the reps and warranties, but they were still locking down the final details, so the deal is pending right now."

78. How did you narrow down potential targets (or potential investors)?

For potential targets, focus on financial, industry, and geographical criteria; for potential investors, talk about what they've invested in before, how much synergy or "fit" there is, and whether or not they have complementary portfolio companies (for PE firms).

"We picked potential investors mostly based on size and acquisition activity in our market in the past. There were a lot of healthcare acquisitions recently, but we wanted to focus on firms that were active in the North American market specifically, and ones that had acquired firms worth over $500 million. We looked at some financial sponsors as well but focused on ones that had sizable healthcare companies in their portfolios."

79. Let's say a distressed company approaches you and wants to hire your bank to sell it in a distressed sale. How would the M and A process be different than it would for a healthy company?

1. Timing is often quick since the company needs to sell or else they'll go bankrupt.
2. Sometimes, you'll produce fewer "upfront" marketing materials (Information Memoranda, Management Presentations, etc.) in the interest of speed.
3. Creditors often initiate the process rather than the company itself.
4. Unlike normal M and A deals, distressed sales can't "fail"; they result in a sale, a bankruptcy, or sometimes a restructuring.

80. Normally, in a sell-side M and A process, you always want to have multiple bidders to increase competition. Is there any reason they'd be especially important in a distressed sale?

Yes, in a distressed sale, you have almost no negotiating leverage because you represent a company that's about to die. The only real way to improve the price for your client is to have multiple bidders.

81. The two basic ways you can buy a company are through a stock purchase and an asset purchase. What's the difference, and what would a buyer in a distressed sale prefer? What about the seller?

In a stock purchase, you acquire 100% of a company's shares as well as all its assets and liabilities (on and off-balance sheet). In an asset purchase, you acquire only certain assets of a company and assume only certain liabilities, so you can pick and choose exactly what you're getting.

Companies typically use asset purchases for divestitures, distressed M&A, and smaller private companies; anything large, public, and healthy generally needs to be acquired via a stock purchase.

A buyer almost always prefers an asset purchase so that it can avoid the assumption of unknown liabilities. There are also tax advantages for the buyer.

A distressed seller almost always prefers a stock purchase so it can be rid of all its liabilities and because it gets taxed more heavily when selling assets vs. selling the entire business.

82. Sometimes, a distressed sale does not end in a conventional stock/asset purchase. What are some other possible outcomes?

Other possible outcomes:

- foreclosure (either official or unofficial)
- general assignment (faster alternative to bankruptcy)
- section 363 asset sale (a faster, less risky version of a normal asset sale)
- chapter 11 bankruptcy
- chapter 7 bankruptcy

83. Normally, M and A processes are kept confidential. Is there any reason why a distressed company would want to announce the involvement of a banker in a sale process?

This happens even outside distressed sales—generally, the company does it if they want more bids/want to increase competition and drive a higher purchase price.

84. Are shareholders likely to receive any compensation in a distressed sale or bankruptcy?

Technically, the answer is "it depends," but practically speaking, most of the time, the answer is "no."

If a company is truly distressed, the value of its debts and obligations most likely exceeds the value of its assets, so equity investors rarely get much out of a bankruptcy or distressed sale, especially when it ends in liquidation.

85. What's the difference between a Distressed M and A deal and a Restructuring deal?

"Restructuring" is one possible outcome of a distressed M and A deal. A company can be "distressed" for many reasons, but the solution is not always to restructure its debt obligations; it might declare bankruptcy, it might liquidate and sell off its assets, or sell 100% of itself to another company.

"Restructuring" just refers to what happens when the distressed company in question decides it wants to change its debt obligations so that it can better repay them in the future.

Technical Questions and Answers

Accounting Q and A

In terms of technical questions, accounting is almost a certainty, so make sure you dust off your accounting textbook in your junior year and start reviewing. All investment bankers must be able to read financial statements and be able to broadly understand the cascading effects of the three financial statements (cash flow, income, and balance sheet).

For someone with either finance experience or an accounting/finance undergrad, expect more advanced questions. If you don't have a business background, make sure you understand the terms and the basics (credit/debit, three statements).

86. Walk me through the three financial statements.

"The three major financial statements are the income statement, balance sheet and cash flow statement.

The income statement gives the company's revenue and expenses and goes down to net income, the final line on the statement.

The balance sheet shows the company's assets; its resources, such as cash, inventory, and PP&E, as well as its Liabilities, such as debt and accounts payable, and shareholders' equity. Assets must equal liabilities plus shareholders' equity.

The cash flow statement begins with net income, adjusts for non-cash expenses and working capital changes, and then lists cash flow from investing and financing activities; at the end, you see the company's net change in cash."

87. How do the three statements link together?

"To tie the statements together, net income from the income statement flows into shareholders' equity on the balance sheet, and into the top line of the cash flow statement.

Changes to balance sheet items appear as working capital changes on the cash flow statement, and investing and financing activities affect balance sheet items such as PP&E, debt, and shareholders' equity. The cash and shareholders' equity items on the balance sheet act as "plugs," with cash flowing in from the final line on the cash flow statement."

88. If I were stranded on a desert island, I only had 1 statement, and I wanted to review the overall health of a company. Which statement would I use and why?

You would use the cash flow statement because it gives a true picture of how much cash the company is actually generating, independent of all the non-cash expenses you might have. And that's the #1 thing you care about when analyzing the overall financial health of any business; its cash flow.

89. Let's say I could only look at two statements to assess a company's prospects. Which two would I use and why?

You would pick the income statement and balance sheet because you can create the Cash Flow Statement from both of those (assuming, of course, that you have "before" and "after" versions of the balance sheet that correspond to the same period the income statement is tracking).

90. Walk me through how depreciation going up by $10 would affect the statements. Income statement: Operating Income would decline by $10, and assuming a 40% tax rate,

Net income would go down by $6.

Cash flow statement: The net income at the top goes down by $6, but the $10 depreciation is a non-cash expense that gets added back, so overall cash flow from operations goes up by $4. There are no changes elsewhere, so the overall net change in cash goes up by $4.

Balance sheet: Plants, property, and equipment goes down by $10 on the assets side because of the depreciation, and cash is up by $4 from the changes on the cash flow statement.

Overall, assets is down by $6. Since net income fell by $6 as well, shareholders' equity on the Liabilities and shareholders' equity side is down by $6 and both sides of the balance sheet balance.

Note: With this type of question, I always recommend going in the order:

1. Income statement
2. Cash flow statement
3. Balance sheet

This is so you can check yourself at the end and make sure the balance sheet balances. Remember that an asset going up decreases your cash flow, whereas a liability going up increases your cash flow.

91. If depreciation is a non-cash expense, why does it affect the cash balance?

Although depreciation is a non-cash expense, it is tax deductible. Since taxes are a cash expense, depreciation affects cash by reducing the amount of taxes you pay.

92. Where does depreciation usually show up on the income statement?

It could be in a separate line item, or it could be embedded in the Cost of Goods Sold or Operating Expenses—every company does it differently. Note that the end result for accounting questions is the same: depreciation always reduces pre-tax income.

93. What happens when accrued compensation goes up by $10?

For this question, confirm that the accrued compensation is now being recognized as an expense (as opposed to just changing non-accrued to accrued compensation).

Assuming that's the case, operating expenses on the income statement go up by $10, pre-tax income falls by $10, and net income falls by $6 (assuming a 40% tax rate).

On the cash flow statement, net income is down by $6, and accrued compensation will increase cash flow by $10, so overall cash flow from operations is up by $4, and the net change in cash at the bottom is up by $4.

On the balance sheet, cash is up by $4 as a result, so assets are up by $4. On the liabilities and equity side, accrued compensation is a liability, so liabilities are up by $10, and retained earnings are down by $6 due to the Net income, so both sides balance.

94. What happens when inventory goes up by $10, assuming you pay for it with cash?

No changes to the income statement.

On the cash flow statement, inventory is an asset that decreases your cash operations; it goes down by $10, as does the net change in cash at the bottom.

On the balance sheet under assets, inventory is up by $10, but cash is down by $10, so the changes cancel out, and assets still equal liabilities and shareholders' equity.

95. How is GAAP accounting different from tax accounting?

1. GAAP is accrual-based, but tax is cash-based.

2. GAAP uses straight-line depreciation or a few other methods, whereas tax accounting is different (accelerated depreciation).

3. GAAP is more complex and more accurately tracks assets/liabilities, whereas tax accounting is only concerned with revenue/expenses in the current period and what income tax you owe.

96. What are deferred tax assets/liabilities, and how do they arise?

They arise because of temporary differences between what a company can deduct for cash tax purposes vs. what they can deduct for book-tax purposes.

Deferred tax liabilities arise when you have a tax expense on the income statement but haven't actually paid that tax in cold, hard cash yet; deferred tax assets arise when you pay taxes in cash but haven't expensed them on the income statement yet.

The most common way they occur is with asset write-ups and write-downs in M and A deal, an asset write-up will produce a deferred tax liability, while a write-down will produce a deferred tax asset (see the Merger Model section for more on this).

97. Walk me through how you create a revenue model for a company.

There are two ways you could do this: a bottoms-up build and a tops-down build.

- **Bottoms-up:** Start with individual products/customers, estimate the average sale value or customer value, and then the growth rate in sales and sale values to tie everything together.
- **Tops-down:** Start with "big-picture" metrics like overall market size, then estimate the company's market share and how that will change in coming years, and multiply to get to their revenue.

Of these two methods, bottoms-up is more common and is taken more seriously because estimating "big-picture" numbers is almost impossible.

98. Walk me through how you create an expense model for a company.

To do a true bottoms-up build, you start with each different department of a company, the # of employees in each, the average salary, bonuses, and benefits, and then make assumptions on those going forward.

Usually, you assume that the number of employees is tied to revenue, and then you assume growth rates for salary, bonuses, benefits, and other metrics.

The Cost of Goods Sold should be directly tied to revenue, and each "unit" produced should incur an expense.

Other items such as rent, Capital Expenditures, and miscellaneous expenses are either linked to the company's internal plans for building expansion plans (if they have them) or to revenue for a simpler model.

99. Let's say we're trying to create these models but don't have enough information, or the company doesn't tell us enough in its filings. What do we do?

Use estimates. For the revenue, if you don't have enough information to look at separate product lines or divisions of the company, you can just assume a simple growth rate into future years.

For the expenses, if you don't have employee-level information, then you can just assume that major expenses like SG&A are a percent of revenue and carry that assumption forward.

100. Walk me through the major items in shareholders' equity.

Common items include:

- **Common stock:** Simply the par value of however much stock the company has issued.
- **Retained earnings:** How much of the company's net income it has "saved up" over time.
- **Additional paid in capital:** This keeps track of how much stock-based compensation has been issued and how much new stock employees exercising options have created. It also includes how much over-par value a company raises in an IPO or other equity offering.
- **Treasury stock:** The dollar amount of shares that the company has bought back.
- **Accumulated other comprehensive income:** This is a "catch-all" that includes other items that don't fit anywhere else, like the effect of foreign currency exchange rates changing.

101. Walk me through what flows into retained earnings.

Retained earnings = Old retained earnings balance + net income – dividends issued. If you're calculating retained earnings for the current year, take last year's retained.

Earnings number, add this year's net income, and subtract however much the company paid out in dividends.

102. What's the difference between capital leases and operating leases?

Operating leases are used for short-term leasing of equipment and property and do not involve ownership of anything. Operating lease expenses show up as operating expenses on the income statement.

Capital leases are used for longer-term items and give the lessee ownership rights; they depreciate and incur interest payments and are counted as debt.

A lease is a capital lease if any one of the following four conditions is true:

1. If there's a transfer of ownership at the end of the term.
2. If there's an option to purchase the asset at a bargain price at the end of the term.
3. If the term of the lease is greater than 75% of the useful life of the asset.
4. If the present value of the lease payments is greater than 90% of the asset's fair market value.

103. What is the statement of shareholders' equity, and why do we use it?

This statement shows everything we went through above—the major items that comprise shareholders' equity, and how we arrived at each of them using the numbers elsewhere in the statement.

You don't use it too much, but it can be helpful for analyzing companies with unusual stock-based compensation and stock option situations.

104. What are examples of non-recurring charges we need to add back to a company's EBIT/EBITDA when looking at its financial statements?

- restructuring charges
- goodwill impairment

- asset write-downs
- bad debt expenses
- legal expenses
- disaster expenses
- change in accounting procedures

Note that to be an "add-back" or "non-recurring" charge for EBITDA/EBIT purposes, it needs to affect operating income on the income statement. So, if you have one of these charges "below the line," then you do not add it back for the EBITDA/EBIT calculation.

Also note that you do add back depreciation, Amortization, and sometimes stock-based compensation for EBITDA/EBIT, but that these are not "non-recurring charges" because all companies have them every year—these are just non-cash charges.

105. How do you project balance sheet items like accounts receivable and accrued expenses in a 3-statement model?

Normally, you make very simple assumptions here and assume these are percentages of revenue, operating expenses, or cost of goods sold. Examples:

- **Accounts receivable:** % of revenue.
- **Deferred revenue:** % of revenue.
- **Accounts payable:** % of COGS.
- **Accrued expenses:** % of operating expenses or SG&A.

Then you either carry the same percentages across in future years or assume slight changes depending on the company.

Enterprise and Equity Value Q and A

For the most part, enterprise value and equity value questions are straightforward. Just make sure you know all the relevant formulas and understand concepts like the treasury stock method for calculating diluted shares.

106. Why do we look at both enterprise value and equity value?

Enterprise value represents the value of the company that is attributable to all investors; equity value only represents the portion available to shareholders (equity investors).

You look at both because equity value is the number the public-at-large sees, while enterprise value represents its true value.

107. When looking at an acquisition of a company, do you pay more attention to enterprise or equity value?

Enterprise value because that's how much an acquirer really "pays" and includes the often mandatory debt repayment.

108. What's the formula for enterprise value?

EV = Equity Value + Debt + Preferred Stock + Minority Interest - Cash

This formula does not tell the whole story and can get more complex—see the advanced questions. Most of the time, you can get away with stating this formula in an interview, though.

109. Why do you need to add minority interest to enterprise value?

Whenever a company owns over 50% of another company, it is required to report the financial performance of the other company as part of its own performance.

So even though it doesn't own 100%, it reports 100% of the majority-owned subsidiary's financial performance.

In keeping with the "apples-to-apples" theme, you must add minority interest to get to enterprise value so that your numerator and denominator both reflect 100% of the majority-owned subsidiary.

110. How do you calculate fully diluted shares?

Take the basic share count and add in the dilutive effect of stock options and any other dilutive securities, such as warrants, convertible debt, or convertible preferred stock.

To calculate the dilutive effect of options, you use the treasury stock method (detail on this below).

111. Let's say a company has 100 shares outstanding at a share price of $10 each. It also has 10 options outstanding at an exercise price of $5 each. What is its fully diluted equity value?

Its basic equity value is $1,000 (100 * $10 = $1,000). To calculate the dilutive effect of the options, first, you note that the options are all "in-the-money"—their exercise price is less than the current share price.

When these options are exercised, there will be 10 new shares created, so the share count is now 110 rather than 100.

However, that doesn't tell the whole story. In order to exercise the options, we had to "pay" the company $5 for each option (the exercise price).

As a result, it now has $50 in additional cash, which it now uses to buy back 5 of the new shares we created.

So, the fully diluted share count is 105, and the fully diluted equity value is $1,050.

112. Let's say a company has 100 shares outstanding at a share price of $10 each. It also has 10 options outstanding at an exercise price of $15 each. What is its fully diluted equity value?

$1,000. In this case, the options' exercise price is above the current share price, so they have no dilutive effect.

113. Why do you subtract cash in the formula for enterprise value? Is that always accurate?

The "official" reason: cash is subtracted because it's considered a non-operating asset and because equity value implicitly accounts for it.

The way I think about it: In an acquisition, the buyer would "get" the cash of the seller, so it effectively pays less for the company based on how large its cash balance is.

Remember, enterprise value tells us how much you'd really have to "pay" to acquire another company.

It's not always accurate because, technically, you should be subtracting only excess cash—the amount of cash a company has above the minimum cash it requires to operate.

114. Is it always accurate to add debt to equity value when calculating enterprise value?

In most cases, yes, because the terms of a debt agreement usually say that debt must be refinanced in an acquisition. And in most cases, a buyer will pay off a seller's debt, so it is accurate to say that any debt "adds" to the purchase price.

However, there could always be exceptions where the buyer does not pay off the debt. These are rare, and I've personally never seen it but once again, "never say never" applies.

115. Could a company have a negative enterprise value? What would that mean?

Yes. It means that the company has an extremely large cash balance or an extremely low market capitalization (or both). You see it with:

1. Companies on the brink of bankruptcy.
2. Financial institutions, such as banks, that have large cash balances.

These days, there's a lot of overlap in these two categories

116. Could a company have a negative equity value? What would that mean?

No. This is not possible because you cannot have a negative share count and you cannot have a negative share price.

117. Why do we add preferred stock to get to enterprise value?

Preferred Stock pays out a fixed dividend, and preferred stockholders also have a higher claim to a company's assets than equity investors do. As a result, it is seen as more similar to debt than common stock.

118. How do you account for convertible bonds in the enterprise value formula?

If the convertible bonds are in-the-money, meaning that the conversion price of the bonds is below the current share price, then you count them as additional dilution to the

Equity value: if they're out-of-the-money, then you count the face value of the convertibles as part of the company's Debt.

119. A company has 1 million shares outstanding at a value of $100 per share. It also has $10 million of convertible bonds, with a par value of $1,000 and a conversion price of $50. How do I calculate diluted shares outstanding?

This gets confusing because of the different units involved. First, note that these convertible bonds are in-the-money because the company's share price is $100, but the conversion price is $50. So, we count them as additional shares rather than debt.

Next, we need to divide the value of the convertible bonds—$10 million—by the par value—$1,000—to figure out how many individual bonds we get: $10 million/$1,000 = 10,000 convertible bonds.

Next, we need to figure out how many shares this number represents. The number of shares per bond is the par value divided by the conversion price: $1,000/$50 = 20 shares per bond.

So, we have 200,000 new shares (20 * 10,000) created by the convertibles, giving us 1.2 million diluted shares outstanding.

We do not use the treasury stock method with convertibles because the company is not "receiving" any cash from us.

120. What's the difference between equity value and shareholders' equity?

Equity value is the market value, and shareholders' equity is the book value. Equity value can never be negative because shares outstanding and share prices can never be negative, whereas shareholders' equity could be any value. For healthy companies, equity value usually far exceeds shareholders' equity.

121. Are there any problems with the enterprise value formula you just gave me?

Yes, it's too simple. There are lots of other things you need to add to the formula with real companies:

- **Net operating losses:** Should be valued and arguably added in, similar to cash.
- **Long-term investments:** These should be counted, similar to cash.
- **Equity investments** Any investments in other companies should also be added in, similar to cash (though they might be discounted).
- **Capital leases:** Like debt, these have interest payments, so they should be added in like debt.

- **(Some) operating leases:** Sometimes, you need to convert operating leases to capital leases and add them as well.

- **Pension obligations:** Sometimes, these are counted as debt as well.

A more "correct" formula would be: Enterprise Value = Equity Value - Cash + Debt + Preferred Stock + Minority Interest - NOLs - Investments + Capital Leases + Pension Obligations.

In interviews, usually, you can get away with saying, "Enterprise Value = Equity Value – Cash + Debt + Preferred Stock + Minority Interest"

122. Should you use the book value or market value of each item when calculating enterprise value?

Technically, you should use market value for everything. In practice, however, you usually use market value only for the equity value portion because it's almost impossible to establish market values for the rest of the items in the formula, so you just take the numbers from the company's Balance Sheet.

123. What percentage dilution in equity value is "too high?"

There's no strict "rule" here, but most bankers would say that anything over 10% is odd.

If your basic equity value is $100 million and the diluted equity value is $115 million, you might want to check your calculations; it's not necessarily wrong, but over 10% dilution is unusual for most companies.

Valuation Q and A

These days, you need to have a better-than-average understanding of valuation. Forget about just knowing the three methodologies—you need to understand how and why they're used, which ones produce the highest or lowest values, and also keep in mind some exceptions to each "rule."

These more advanced questions cover industry-specific valuation in more detail, as well as scenarios like IPO valuation, M and A premiums, and future share price analysis that are not likely to come up in entry-level interviews but could come up if you're going for more advanced positions.

124. What are the three major valuation methodologies?

Comparable Companies, Precedent Transactions, and Discounted Cash Flow Analysis.

125. Rank the three valuation methodologies from highest to lowest expected value.

Trick question: there is no ranking that always holds. In general, precedent transactions will be higher than comparable companies due to the control premium built into acquisitions. Beyond that, a DCF could go either way, and it's best to say that it's more variable than other methodologies. Often, it produces the highest value, but it can produce the lowest value as well, depending on your assumptions.

126. When would you not use a DCF in a valuation?

You do not use a DCF if the company has unstable or unpredictable cash flows (tech or bio-tech startup) or when debt and working capital serve a fundamentally different role. For example, banks and financial institutions do not re-invest debt, and working capital is a huge part of their balance sheets, so you wouldn't use a DCF for such companies.

127. What other valuation methodologies are there?

Other methodologies include:

- **Liquidation valuation:** Valuing a company's assets, assuming they are sold off, and then subtracting liabilities to determine how much capital, if any, equity investors receive

- **Replacement value:** Valuing a company based on the cost of replacing its assets

- **LBO analysis:** Determining how much a PE firm could pay for a company to hit a "target" IRR, usually in the 20-25% range

128. When would you use a liquidation valuation?

This is most common in bankruptcy scenarios and is used to see whether equity shareholders will receive any capital after the company's debts have been paid off. It is often used to advise struggling businesses on whether it's better to sell off assets separately or to try to sell the entire company.

129. When would you use a sum of the parts?

This is most often used when a company has completely different, unrelated divisions—a conglomerate like General Electric, for example.

If you have a plastics division, a TV and entertainment division, an energy division, a consumer financing division. Suppose you have a plastics division, a TV and entertainment division, an energy division, a consumer financing division, and a technology division. In that case, you should not use the same set of comparable companies and precedent transactions for the entire company.

Instead, you should use different sets for each division, value each one separately, and then add them together to get the combined value.

130. When do you use an LBO analysis as part of your valuation?

Obviously, you use this whenever you're looking at a leveraged buyout, but it is also used to establish how much a private equity firm could pay, which is usually lower than what companies will pay.

131. What are the most common multiples used in valuation?

The most common multiples are EV/revenue, EV/EBITDA, EV/EBIT, P/E (share price/earnings per share), and P/BV (share price/book value).

132. What are some examples of industry-specific multiples?

Technology (internet): EV/unique visitors, EV/page views

Retail/airlines: EV/EBITDAR (earnings before interest, taxes, depreciation, Amortization & rent)

Energy: P/MCFE, P/MCFE/D (MCFE = 1 million cubic foot equivalent, MCFE/D = MCFE per day), P/NAV (share price/net asset value)

Real estate investment trusts (REITs): Price/FFO, Price/AFFO (funds from operations, adjusted funds from operations)

Technology and energy should be straightforward—you're looking at traffic and energy reserves as value drivers rather than revenue or profit.

For retail/airlines, you often remove rent because it is a major expense and one that varies significantly between different types of companies.

For REITs, funds from operations are a common metric that adds back depreciation and subtract gains on the sale of the property. Depreciation is a non-cash yet extremely large expense in real estate, and gains on sales of properties are assumed to be non-recurring, so FFO is viewed as a "normalized" picture of the cash flow the REIT is generating.

133. When you're looking at an industry-specific multiple like EV/scientists or EV/subscribers. Why do you use enterprise value rather than equity value?

You use enterprise value because those scientists or subscribers are "available" to all the investors (both debt and equity) in a company. The same logic doesn't apply to everything, though; you need to think through the multiples and see which investors the particular metric is "available" to.

134. How do you value banks and financial institutions differently from other companies?

You mostly use the same methodologies, except:

- You look at P/E and P/BV (book value) multiples rather than EV/ revenue, EV/ EBITDA, and other "normal" multiples, since banks have unique capital structures.
- You pay more attention to bank-specific metrics like NAV (Net Asset Value), and you might screen companies and precedent transactions based on those instead.
- Rather than a DCF, you use a dividend discount model (DDM), which is similar but is based on the present value of the company's dividends rather than its free cash flows.

You need to use these methodologies and multiples because interest is a critical component of a bank's revenue and because debt is part of its business model rather than just a way to finance acquisitions or expand the business.

135. Walk me through an IPO valuation for a company that's about to go public.

1. Unlike normal valuations, for an IPO valuation, we only care about public company comparables.
2. After picking the public company comparables, we decide on the most relevant multiple use and then estimate our company's enterprise value based on that.
3. Once we have the enterprise value, we work backward to get to equity value and also subtract the IPO proceeds because this is "new" cash.

4. Then, we divide by the total number of shares (old and newly created) to get its per-share price. When people say, "An IPO priced at..." this is what they're referring to.

If you were using P/E or any other "equity value-based multiple" for the multiple in step #2 here, then you would get to equity value instead and then subtract the IPO proceeds from there.

136. I'm looking at financial data for a public company comparable, and it's April (Q2) right now. Walk me through how you would "calendarize" this company's financial statements to show the trailing twelve months as opposed to just the last fiscal year.

The "formula" to calendarize financial statements is as follows: TTM = Most recent fiscal year + newpPartial period—old partial period

So, in the example above, we would take the company's Q1 numbers, add the most recent fiscal year's numbers, and then subtract the Q1 numbers from that most recent fiscal year.

For US companies, you can find these quarterly numbers in the 10-Q; for international companies, they're in the "interim" reports.

137. Walk me through an M and A premiums analysis.

The purpose of this analysis is to look at similar transactions and see the premiums that buyers have paid to sellers' share prices when acquiring them. For example, if a company is trading at $10.00/share and the buyer acquires it for $15.00/share, that's a 50% premium.

1. First, select the precedent transactions based on industry, date (past 2-3 years, for example), and size (example: over $1 billion market cap).

2. For each transaction, get the seller's share price 1 day, 20 days, and 60 days before the transaction was announced (you can also look at even longer intervals, or 30 days, 45 days, etc.).

3. Then, calculate the 1-day premium, 20-day premium, etc., by dividing the per share purchase price by the appropriate share prices on each day.

4. Get the medians for each set, and then apply them to your company's current share price, share price 20 days ago, etc., to estimate how much of a premium a buyer might pay for it.

138. Walk me through a future share price analysis.

The purpose of this analysis is to project what a company's share price might be 1 or 2 years from now and then discount it back to its present value.

1. Get the median historical (usually TTM) P/E of your public company comparables.
2. Apply this P/E multiple to your company's 1-year forward or 2-year forward projected EPS to get its implied future share price.
3. Then, discount this back to its present value by using a discount rate in line with the company's cost of equity figures.

You normally look at a range of P/E multiples as well as a range of discount rates for this type of analysis and make a sensitivity table with these as inputs.

139. Both M and A premiums analysis and precedent transactions involve looking at previous M and A transactions. What's the difference in how we select them?

- All the sellers in the M&A premiums analysis must be public.
- Usually, we use a broader set of transactions for M and A premiums—we might use fewer than ten precedent transactions, but we might have dozens of M and A premiums. The industry and financial screens are usually less stringent.
- Aside from those, the screening criteria are similar: financial, industry, geography, and date.

140. Walk me through a sum-of-the-parts analysis.

In a Sum-of-the-Parts analysis, you value each division of a company using separate comparables and transactions, get separate multiples, and then add up each division's value to get the total for the company. Example:

We have a manufacturing division with $100 million EBITDA, an entertainment division with $50 million EBITDA, and a consumer goods division with $75 million EBITDA.

We've selected comparable companies and transactions for each division, and the median multiples come out to 5x EBITDA for manufacturing, 8x EBITDA for entertainment, and 4x EBITDA for consumer goods.

Our calculation would be $100 * 5x + $50 * 8x + $75 * 4x = $1.2 billion for the company's total value.

143. How do you value net operating losses and take them into account in a valuation?

You value NOLs based on how much they'll save the company in taxes in future years and then take the present value of the sum of tax savings in future years. Two ways to assess the tax savings in future years:

1. Assume that a company can use its NOLs to completely offset its taxable income until the NOLs run out.
2. In an acquisition scenario, use section 382 and multiply the adjusted long-term rate (http://pmstax.com/afr/exemptAFR.shtml) by the equity purchase price of the seller to determine the maximum allowed NOL usage in each year, and then use that to figure out the offset to taxable income.

You might consider NOLs in a valuation, but you rarely include them. If you did, they would be similar to cash. You would subtract NOLs to go from Equity Value to Enterprise Value, and vice versa.

144. I have a set of public company comparables and need to get the projections from equity research. How do I select which report to use?

This varies by bank and group, but two common methods:

1. You pick the report with the most detailed information.
2. You pick the report with numbers in the middle of the range.

Note that you do not pick reports based on which bank they're coming from. So, if you're at Goldman Sachs, you would not pick all Goldman Sachs equity research; in fact, that would be bad because then your valuation would not be objective.

145. I have a set of precedent transactions, but I'm missing information like EBITDA for a lot of the companies. How can I find it if it's not available via public sources?

1. Search online and see if you can find press releases or articles in the financial press with these numbers.
2. Failing that, look at equity research for the buyer around the time of the transaction and see if any of the analysts estimate the seller's numbers.

3. Also, look at online sources like Capital IQ and Factset and see if any of them disclose numbers or give estimates.

Discounted Cash Flow Q and A

Beyond knowing the basics of how to construct a DCF, you also need to understand concepts such as WACC, cost of equity and the proper discount rates to use depending on the scenario. Interviewers also like to ask about terminal value—how you calculate it, the advantages and disadvantages of different methods, and signs that it's "too high."

146. Walk me through a DCF.

"A DCF values a company based on the present value of its cash flows and the present value of its terminal value. First, you project out a company's financials using assumptions for revenue growth, expenses, and working capital; then you get down to free cash flow for each year, which you then sum up and discount to a net present value, based on your discount rate—usually the weighted average cost of capital. Once you have the present value of the cash flows, you determine the company's terminal value, using either the multiples method or the gordon growth method, and then also discount that back to its net present value using WACC. Finally, you add the two together to determine the company's enterprise value."

147. Walk me through how you get from revenue to free cash flow in the projections.

Subtract COGS and operating expenses to get to operating income (EBIT). Then, multiply by (1 – Tax Rate), add back depreciation and other non-cash charges, and subtract capital expenditures and the change in working capital. Note: This gets you to unlevered free cash flow since you went off EBIT rather than EBT. You might want to confirm that this is what the interviewer is asking for.

148. What's an alternate way to calculate free cash flow aside from taking net income, adding back depreciation, and subtracting changes in operating assets/liabilities and CapEx?

Take cash flow from operations and subtract CapEx—that gets you to levered cash flow. To get to Unlevered Cash Flow, you then need to add back the tax-adjusted.

Interest expense and subtract the tax-adjusted interest income.

149. Why do you use 5 or 10 years for DCF projections?

That's usually about as far as you can reasonably predict in the future. Less than 5 years would be too short to be useful, and over 10 years is too difficult to predict for most companies.

150. What do you usually use for the discount rate?

Normally, you use WACC (Weighted Average Cost of Capital), though you might also use cost of equity depending on how you've set up the DCF.

151. How do you calculate WACC?

The formula is: Cost of Equity * (% Equity) + Cost of Debt * (% Debt) * (1 – Tax Rate) + Cost of Preferred * (% Preferred).

In all cases, the percentages refer to how much of the company's capital structure is taken up by each component.

For cost of equity, you can use the Capital Asset Pricing Model (CAPM, see the next question), and for the others, you usually look at comparable companies/debt issuances and the interest rates and yields issued by similar companies to get estimates.

152. How do you calculate the cost of equity?

Cost of Equity = Risk-Free Rate + Beta * Equity Risk Premium

The risk-free rate represents how much a 10-year or 20-year US treasury should yield;

Beta is calculated based on the "riskiness" of comparable companies and the equity

Risk premium is the % by which stocks are expected to outperform "risk-less" assets.

Normally, you pull the equity risk premium from a publication called Ibbotson's.

Note: This formula does not tell the whole story. Depending on the bank and how precise you want to be, you could also add in a "size premium" and "industry premium" to account for how much a company is expected to outperform its peers according to its market cap or industry.

Small company stocks are expected to outperform large company stocks, and certain industries are expected to outperform others, and these premiums reflect these expectations.

153. How do you get to beta in the cost of equity calculation?

You look up the beta for each comparable company (usually on Bloomberg), unlever each one, take the median of the set, and then lever it based on your company's capital structure. Then, you use this levered beta in the cost of equity calculation.

For your reference, the formulas for un-levering and re-levering beta are below:

Un-Levered Beta = Levered beta/(1 + (1 - tax rate) x (Total debt/equity)

Levered Beta = Unlevered beta x (1 + (1 - tax rate) x (Total debt/equity)

155. Why do you have to unlever and relever beta?

Again, keep in mind our "apples-to-apples" theme. When you look up the betas on Bloomberg (or from whatever source you're using) they will be levered to reflect the debt already assumed by each company.

However, each company's capital structure is different, and we want to look at how "risky" a company is regardless of what % debt or equity it has.

To get that, we need to unlever beta each time.

But at the end of the calculation, we need to relever it because we want the beta used in the cost of equity calculation to reflect the true risk of our company, taking into account its capital structure this time.

156. Would you expect a manufacturing company or a technology company to have a higher beta?

A technology company because technology is viewed as a "riskier" industry than manufacturing.

157. Let's say that you use levered free cash flow rather than unlevered free cash flow in your DCF. What is the effect?

Levered free cash flow gives you equity value rather than enterprise value since the cash flow is only available to equity investors (debt investors have already been "paid" with the interest payments).

158. If you use levered free cash flow, what should you use as the discount rate?

You would use the cost of equity rather than WACC since we're not concerned with debt or preferred stock in this case; we're calculating equity value, not enterprise value.

159. How do you calculate the terminal value?

You can either apply an exit multiple to the company's Year 5 EBITDA, EBIT, or Free Cash Flow (Multiples Method), or you can use the Gordon Growth method to estimate its value based on its growth rate into perpetuity.

The formula for Terminal Value using Gordon Growth is: Terminal Value

160. Explain why we would use the mid-year convention in a DCF.

You use it to represent the fact that a company's cash flow does not come 100% at the end of each year; instead, it comes in evenly throughout each year.

In a DCF without a mid-year convention, we would use discount period numbers of 1 for the first year, 2 for the second year, 3 for the third year, and so on.

With the mid-year convention, we would instead use 0.5 for the first year, 1.5 for the second year, 2.5 for the third year, and so on.

161. What discount period numbers would I use for the mid-year convention if I have a stub period; e.g., Q4 of Year 1 – in my DCF?

The rule is that you divide the stub discount period by 2, and then you simply subtract 0.5 from the "normal" discount periods for the future years. Example for a Q4 stub:

Q4 year 1 year 2 year 3 year 4 year 5

Normal discount periods with stubs: 0.25 1.25 2.25 3.25 4.25 5.25

Mid-year discount periods with stubs: 0.125 0.75 1.75 2.75 3.75 4.75

162. How does the terminal value calculation change when we use the mid-year convention?

When you're discounting the terminal value back to the present value, you use different numbers for the discount period depending on whether you're using the multiples.

Method or gordon growth method:

- **Multiples method:** You add 0.5 to the final year discount number to reflect the fact that you're assuming the company gets sold at the end of the year.

- **Gordon growth method:** You should use the final year discount number as is because you are assuming that the cash flows grow into perpetuity and that they are received throughout the year rather than just at the end.

163. If I'm working with a public company in a DCF, how do I calculate its per-share value?

Once you get to Enterprise Value, ADD cash and then subtract debt, preferred stock, and minority interest (and any other debt-like items) to get to Equity Value.

Then, you need to use a circular calculation that takes into account the basic shares outstanding, options, warrants, convertibles, and other dilutive securities. It's circular because the dilution from these depends on the per-share price, but the per-share price depends on number of shares outstanding, which depends on the per-share price.

To resolve this, you need to enable iterative calculations in excel so that it can cycle through to find an approximate per-share price.

164. Walk me through a dividend discount model (DDM) that you would use in place of a normal DCF for financial institutions.

The mechanics are the same as a DCF, but we use dividends rather than free cash flows:

1. Project out the company's earnings down to earnings per share (EPS).

2. Assume a dividend payout ratio, what percentage of the EPS actually gets paid out to shareholders in the form of dividends, based on what the firm has done historically and how much regulatory capital it needs.

3. Use this to calculate dividends over the next 5-10 years.

4. Discount each dividend to its present value based on cost of equity—NOT

    a. WACC—and then sum these up.

5. Calculate terminal value based on P/E and EPS in the final year, and then discount this to its present value based on cost of equity.

6. Sum the present value of the terminal value and the present values of the dividends to get the company's net present per-share value.

165. When you're calculating WACC, let's say that the company has convertible debt. Do you count this as debt when calculating the levered beta for the company?

Trick question. If the convertible debt is in-the-money then you do not count it as debt but instead assume that it contributes to dilution, so the company's equity Value is higher. If it's out-of-the-money, then you count it as debt and use the interest rate on the convertible for cost of debt.

166. We're creating a DCF for a company that is planning to buy a factory for $100 in cash (no debt or other financing) in year 4. Currently, the present value of its enterprise value, according to the DCF, is $200. How would we change the DCF to account for the factory purchase, and what would our new enterprise value be?

In this scenario, you would add CapEx spending of $100 in year 4 of the DCF, which would reduce free cash flow for that year by $100. The enterprise value, in turn, would fall by the present value of that $100 decrease in free cash flow.

The actual math here is messy, but you would calculate the present value by dividing $100 by (1 + Discount Rate^4)—the "4" just represents year 4 here. Then, you would subtract this amount from the Enterprise Value.

Merger Model Q and A

You don't need to understand merger models as well as an M and A banker does, but you do need to do more than just the basics, especially if you've had a finance internship or full-time job before.

It's important to know the effects of an acquisition and understand concepts such as synergies and why Goodwill & Other Intangibles actually get created.

One thing that's not important? Walking through how all three statements are affected by an acquisition. In 99% of cases, you only care about the income statement in a merger model (despite rumors to the contrary).

167. Walk me through a basic merger model.

"A merger model is used to analyze the financial profiles of 2 companies, the purchase price, and how the purchase is made, and determines whether the buyer's EPS increases or decreases.

Step 1 is making assumptions about the acquisition—the price and whether it was cash, stock, or debt, or some combination of those. Next, you determine the valuations and shares outstanding of the buyer and seller and project out an Income Statement for each one.

Finally, you combine the income statements, adding up line items such as revenue and operating expenses, and adjusting for foregone interest in cash and interest paid on debt in the combined pre-tax income line; you apply the buyer's Tax Rate to get the combined net income, and then divide by the new share count to determine the combined EPS."

168. What's the difference between a merger and an acquisition?

There's always a buyer and a seller in any M and A deal—the difference between "merger" and "acquisition" is more semantic than anything. In a merger, the companies are close to the same size, whereas in an acquisition, the buyer is significantly larger.

169. Why would a company want to acquire another company?

Several possible reasons:

- The buyer wants to gain market share by buying a competitor.
- The buyer needs to grow more quickly and sees an acquisition as a way to do that.
- The buyer believes the seller is undervalued.
- The buyer wants to acquire the seller's customers so it can up-sell and cross-sell to them.
- The buyer thinks the seller has a critical technology, intellectual property, or some other "secret sauce" it can use to significantly enhance its business.
- The buyer believes it can achieve significant synergies and therefore, make the deal accretive for its shareholders.

170. Why would an acquisition be dilutive?

An acquisition is dilutive if the additional amount of net income the seller contributes is not enough to offset the buyer's foregone interest on cash, additional interest paid on debt, and the effects of issuing additional shares.

Acquisition effects, such as amortization of intangibles; can also make an acquisition dilutive.

171. Is there a rule of thumb for calculating whether an acquisition will be accretive or dilutive?

If the deal involves just cash and debt, you can sum up the interest expense for debt and the foregone interest on cash, then compare it against the seller's pre-tax income.

And if it's an all-stock deal, you can use a shortcut to assess whether it is accretive (see question #5).

But if the deal involves cash, stock, and debt, there is no quick rule of thumb you can use unless you are lightning-fast with mental math.

172. A company with a higher P/E acquires one with a lower P/E, is this accretive or dilutive?

Trick question. You can't tell unless you also know that it's an all-stock deal. If it's an all-cash or all-debt deal, the P/E multiples of the buyer and seller don't matter because no stock is being issued.

Sure, generally getting more earnings for less is good and is more likely to be accretive but there's no hard-and-fast rule unless it's an all-stock deal.

173. What is the rule of thumb for assessing whether an M and A deal will be accretive or dilutive?

In an all-stock deal, if the buyer has a higher P/E than the seller, it will be accretive; if the buyer has a lower P/E, it will be dilutive.

On an intuitive level, if you're paying more for earnings than what the market values your own earnings at, you can guess that it will be dilutive; and likewise, if you're paying less for earnings than what the market values your own earnings at, you can guess that it would be accretive.

174. What are the complete effects of an acquisition?

1. **Foregone interest on cash:** The buyer loses the Interest it would have otherwise earned if it used cash for the acquisition.

2. **Additional interest in debt:** The buyer pays additional interest expense if it uses debt.

3. **Additional shares outstanding:** If the buyer pays with stock, it must issue additional shares.

4. **Combined financial statements:** After the acquisition, the seller's financials are added to the buyer's.

5. **Creation of Goodwill and other intangibles:** These balances sheet items that represent a "premium" paid to a company's "fair value" also get created.

Note: There's actually more than this (see the advanced questions), but this is usually sufficient to mention in interviews.

175. If a company were capable of paying 100% in cash for another company, why would it choose NOT to do so?

It might be saving its cash for something else or it might be concerned about running low if business takes a turn for the worst; its stock may also be trading at an all-time high and it might be eager to use that instead. In finance terms, this would be considered "more expensive" but a lot of executives value having a safety cushion in the form of a large cash balance.

176. Why would a strategic acquirer typically be willing to pay more for a company than a private equity firm would?

Because the strategic acquirer can realize revenue and cost synergies that the private equity firm cannot unless it combines the company with a complementary portfolio company. Those synergies boost the effective valuation for the target company.

177. What's the difference between purchase accounting and pooling accounting in an M&A deal?

In purchase accounting, the seller's shareholders' equity number is wiped out and the premium paid over that value is recorded as goodwill on the combined balance sheet post-acquisition. In pooling accounting, you simply combine the 2 shareholders' equity numbers rather than worrying about goodwill and the related items that get created.

There are specific requirements for using pooling accounting, so in 99% of M&A deals, you will use purchase accounting.

178. Walk me through a concrete example of how to calculate revenue synergies.

"Let's say that Microsoft is going to acquire Yahoo. Yahoo makes money from search advertising online, and they make a certain amount of revenue per search (RPS). Let's say this RPS is $0.10 right now. If Microsoft acquired it, we might assume that they could boost this RPS by $0.01 or $0.02 because of their superior monetization. So, to calculate the additional revenue from this synergy, we would multiply this $0.01 or $0.02 by Yahoo's total # of searches, get the total additional revenue, and then select a margin on it to determine how much flow through to the combined company's Operating Income."

179. Walk me through an example of how to calculate expense synergies.

"Let's say that Microsoft still wants to acquire Yahoo!. Microsoft has 5,000 SG&A-related employees, whereas Yahoo has around 1,000. Microsoft calculates that post-transaction, it will only need about 200 of Yahoo's SG&A employees, and its existing employees can take over the rest of the work. To calculate the operating expenses the combined company would save, we would multiply these 800 employees Microsoft is going to fire post-transaction by their average salary."

180. Why do deferred tax liabilities (DTLs) and deferred tax assets (DTAs) get created in M&A deals?

These get created when you write up assets—both tangible and intangible—and when you write down assets in a transaction. An asset write-up creates a deferred tax liability, and an asset write-down creates a deferred tax asset.

You write down and write up assets because their book value—what's on the balance sheet—often differs substantially from their "fair market value."

An asset write-up creates a deferred tax liability because you'll have a higher depreciation expense on the new asset, which means you save on taxes in the short-term, but eventually, you'll have to pay them back, hence the liability. The opposite applies for an asset write-down and a deferred tax asset.

LBO Q and A

The field is wide open when you get to questions on leveraged buyouts and LBO models. You need to know the basics, but it's also important to understand how different variables affect the output and how and why a PE firm would structure a deal in a certain way.

You're more likely to get these types of questions if you've already had a banking internship or if you've worked in a group like financial sponsors that work extensively with PE firms.

But even if neither of those applies to you, it's still better to be over-prepared.

181. Walk me through a basic LBO model.

"In an LBO model, step 1 is making assumptions about the purchase price, debt/equity ratio, interest rate on debt and other variables; you might also assume something about the company's operations, such as Revenue Growth or Margins, depending on how much information you have.

Step 2 is to create a source and uses section, which shows how you finance the transaction and what you use the capital for; this also tells you how much investor equity is required.

Step 3 is to adjust the company's balance sheet for the new debt and equity figures and also add in Goodwill and Other Intangibles on the assets side to make everything balance.

In Step 4, you project out the company's income statement, balance Sheet and cash flow statement, and determine how much debt is paid off each year based on the available cash flow and the required interest payments.

Finally, in step 5, you make assumptions about the exit after several years, usually assuming an EBITDA exit multiple, and calculate the return based on how much equity is returned to the firm."

182. Why would you use leverage when buying a company?

To boost your return.

Remember, any debt you use in an LBO is not "your money"—so if you're paying $5 billion for a company, it's easier to earn a high return on $2 billion of your own money and $3 billion borrowed from elsewhere vs. $3 billion of your own money and $2 billion of borrowed money.

A secondary benefit is that the firm also has more capital available to purchase other companies because they've used leverage.

183. What variables impact an LBO model the most?

Purchase and exit multiples have the biggest impact on the returns of a model. After that, the amount of leverage (debt) used also has a significant impact, followed by operational characteristics such as revenue growth and EBITDA margins.

184. How do you pick purchase multiples and exit multiples in an LBO model?

The same way you do it anywhere else: you look at what comparable companies are trading at and what multiples similar LBO transactions have had. As always, you also show a range of purchase and exit multiples using sensitivity tables.

Sometimes, you set purchase and exit multiples based on a specific IRR target that you're trying to achieve—but this is just for valuation purposes if you're using an LBO model to value the company.

185. What is an "ideal" candidate for an LBO?

"Ideal" candidates have stable and predictable cash flows, low-risk businesses, not much need for ongoing investments such as capital expenditures, as well as an opportunity for expense reductions to boost their margins. A strong management team also helps, as does a base of assets to use as collateral for debt.

The most important part is stable cash flow.

186. How do you use an LBO model to value a company, and why do we sometimes say that it sets the "floor valuation" for the company?

You use it to value a company by setting a targeted IRR (for example, 25%) and then back-solving in Excel to determine what purchase price the PE firm could pay to achieve that IRR.

This is sometimes called a "floor valuation" because PE firms almost always pay less for a company than strategic acquirers would.

187. Give an example of a "real-life" LBO.

The most common example is taking out a mortgage when you buy a house. Here's how the analogy works:

- **Down payment:** Investor equity in an LBO
- **Mortgage:** Debt in an LBO
- **Mortgage interest payments:** Debt interest in an LBO
- **Mortgage repayments:** Debt principal repayments in an LBO
- **Selling the house:** Selling the company/taking it public in an LBO

188. Can you explain how the balance sheet is adjusted in an LBO model?

First, the liabilities and equities side is adjusted—the new debt is added on, and the shareholders' equity is "wiped out" and replaced by however much equity the private equity firm is contributing.

On the assets side, cash is adjusted for any cash used to finance the transaction, and then goodwill and other intangibles are used as a "plug" to make the balance sheet balance.

Depending on the transaction, there could be other effects as well—such as capitalized financing fees added to the assets side.

189. Why are goodwill and other intangibles created in an LBO?

Remember, these both represent the premium paid to the "fair market value" of the company. In an LBO, they act as a "plug" and ensure that the changes to the liabilities and equity side are balanced by changes to the assets side.

190. We saw that a strategic acquirer would usually prefer to pay for another company in cash—if that's the case, why would a PE firm want to use debt in an LBO?

It's a different scenario because:

1. The PE firm does not intend to hold the company for the long term—it usually sells it after a few years, so it is less concerned with the "expense" of cash vs. debt and more concerned about using leverage to boost its returns by reducing the amount of capital it has to contribute upfront.

2. In an LBO, the debt is "owned" by the company, so they assume much of the risk. Whereas in a strategic acquisition, the buyer "owns" the debt, so it is more risky for them.

191. Do you need to project all three statements in an LBO model? Are there any "shortcuts?"

Yes, there are shortcuts, and you don't necessarily need to project all three statements. For example, you do not need to create a full balance sheet—bankers sometimes skip this if they are in a rush.

You do need some form of an income statement, something to track how the debt balances change, and some type of cash flow statement to show how much cash is available to repay debt.

But a full-blown balance sheet is not strictly required, because you can just make assumptions on the net change in working capital rather than looking at each item individually.

192. How would you determine how much debt can be raised in an LBO and how many tranches there would be?

Usually, you would look at comparable LBOs and see the terms of the debt and how many tranches each of them used. You would look at companies in a similar size range and industry and use those criteria to determine the debt your company can raise.

193. Let's say we're analyzing how much debt a company can take on and what the terms of the debt should be. What are reasonable leverage and coverage ratios?

This is completely dependent on the company, the industry, and the leverage and coverage ratios for comparable LBO transactions.

To figure out the numbers, you would look at "debt comps," showing the types, tranches, and terms of debt that similarly sized companies in the industry have used recently.

There are some general rules: for example, you would never lever a company at 50x EBITDA, and even during the bubble, leverage rarely exceeded 5-10x EBITDA.

194. What is the difference between bank debt and high-yield debt?

This is a simplification, but broadly speaking, there are two "types" of debt: "bank debt" and "high-yield debt." There are many differences, but here are a few of the most important ones:

- High-yield debt tends to have higher interest rates than bank debt (hence the name "high-yield").
- High-yield debt interest rates are usually fixed, whereas bank debt interest rates are "floating"; they change based on LIBOR or the Fed interest rate.
- High-yield debt has incurrence covenants, while bank debt has maintenance covenants. The main difference is that incurrence covenants prevent you from doing something (such as selling an asset, buying a factory, etc.), while maintenance covenants require you to maintain a minimum financial performance (for example, the debt/EBITDA ratio must be below 5x at all times).

- Bank debt is usually amortized—the principal must be paid off over time, whereas, with high-yield debt, the entire principal is due at the end (bullet maturity).

Usually, in a sizable leveraged buyout, the PE firm uses both types of debt.

Again, there are many different types of debt; this is a simplification, but it's enough for entry-level interviews.

195. Why might you use bank debt rather than high-yield debt in an LBO?

If the PE firm or the company is concerned about meeting interest payments and wants a lower-cost option, they might use bank debt; they might also use bank debt if they are planning on major expansion or capital expenditures and don't want to be restricted by incurrence covenants.

196. Why would a PE firm prefer high-yield debt instead?

If the PE firm intends to refinance the company at some point or they don't believe their returns are too sensitive to interest payments, they might use high-yield debt. They might also use the high-yield option if they don't have plans for major expansion or selling off the company's assets.

197. Why would a private equity firm buy a company in a "risky" industry, such as technology?

Although technology is more "risky" than other markets, remember that there are mature, cash-flow-stable companies in almost every industry. There are some PE firms that specialize in very specific goals, such as:

- **Industry consolidation:** Buying competitors in a similar market and combining them to increase efficiency and win more customers.

- **Turnarounds:** Taking struggling companies and making them function properly again.

- **Divestitures:** Selling off divisions of a company or taking a division and turning it into a strong stand-alone entity.

So even if a company isn't doing well or seems risky, the firm might buy it if it falls into one of these categories.

198. How could a private equity firm boost its return to an LBO?

1. Lower the purchase price in the model.
2. Raise the exit multiple/exit price.
3. Increase the leverage (debt) used.
4. Increase the company's growth rate (organically or via acquisitions).
5. Increase margins by reducing expenses (cutting employees, consolidating buildings, etc.).

Note that these are all "theoretical" and refer to the model rather than reality—in practice, it's hard to actually implement these.

199. What is meant by the "tax shield" in an LBO?

This means that the interest a firm pays on debt is tax-deductible—so they save money on taxes and, therefore, increase their cash flow as a result of having debt from the LBO.

Note, however, that their cash flow is still lower than it would be without the debt—saving on taxes helps, but the added interest expenses still reduce net income over what it would be for a debt-free company.

200. What is a dividend recapitalization ("dividend recap")?

In a dividend recap, the company takes on new debt solely to pay a special dividend out to the PE firm that bought it.

It would be like if you made your friend take out a personal loan just so he/she could pay you a lump sum of cash with the loan proceeds.

As you might guess, dividend recaps have developed a bad reputation, though they're still commonly used.

www.ingramcontent.com/pod-product-compliance
Ingram Content Group UK Ltd.
Pitfield, Milton Keynes, MK11 3LW, UK
UKHW040021200726
13854UKWH00001B/293